29th May 1997.

DUNBLANE
OUR YEAR OF TEARS

DUNBLANE

OUR YEAR OF TEARS

Peter Samson and Alan Crow

MAINSTREAM
PUBLISHING

EDINBURGH AND LONDON

Copyright © *Sunday Mail,* 1997

All rights reserved

The moral right of the authors has been asserted

First published in Great Britain in 1997 by
MAINSTREAM PUBLISHING COMPANY (EDINBURGH) LTD
7 Albany Street
Edinburgh EH1 3UG

ISBN 1 85158 975 9

A catalogue record for this book is available from the British Library

Paper for this book kindly donated by Precision Publishing Papers Ltd with support from Munkedal AB. Printed on Munken Print Extra.

Manufacturing services sponsored by Butler & Tanner Ltd.

Typeset in Garamond
Printed and bound in Great Britain by
Butler & Tanner Ltd, Frome and London

A PRAYER FOR DUNBLANE

Loving Father,
you have shared the months with us,
you have stood beside us in the sorrow and the struggle.
Lead us now to a better future
where healing, acceptance and peace
shall slowly fill our lives.
Give us your strength in our frail moments,
your presence in the absence we feel,
your rest, that we may rise again to life,
and your home that in death we are not divided.

Colin G. McIntosh
Dunblane Cathedral, March 1997

CONTENTS

ACKNOWLEDGEMENTS

WE wish to express our gratitude to the people who agreed to take part in this project. We thank them for their patience and co-operation. Without them this book would not have been possible.

PHOTO CREDITS

All the main photographs are by Ronnie Anderson and the others are from the *Daily Record* and *Sunday Mail* collections.

A DARK DAY AT DUNBLANE

WEDNESDAY, 13 March 1996 – the day the flower of innocence was crushed before the eyes of the world.

It was the blackest of days. The day when the devil, in the guise of a sick, twisted man, visited the tiny Scottish cathedral city of Dunblane. When his evil work was done, 16 little children lay dead or dying in a school gym hall alongside the body of the teacher they loved and respected. Twelve of their classmates and two teachers lay maimed and bleeding.

And the world wept . . .

The children set off for Dunblane Primary that chilly morning, their tiny shoulders unburdened by the troubles and traumas of the world. They were on their way to a place of fun and laughter; a place where children feel warm and secure, a place of trust.

How could anyone walk into that school with hate in his heart and massacre on his mind?

Many have struggled with the question. Most agree we will never truly know the answer.

As Dunblane's parents were embroiled in the early morning hurly-burly of getting their children ready for school, a madman was making his own preparations in his council flat in nearby Stirling.

As mums combed their loved ones' hair and packed them off to school, wrapped up tightly against the cold, he was preparing his arsenal of guns and ammunition with military precision.

The gunman had picked morning assembly as his target. He knew the school hall would be packed with children and teachers.

But the killer was stopped from carrying out the full horror of his plan. Caught up in a traffic jam, he arrived at the school late, missing assembly by minutes.

But he still had carnage on his mind. He carried out his senseless act of depravity in the school gym. Within three minutes he was dead, his despicable deed done.

News of the massacre spread quickly through the town. 'There's been a shooting incident at the school,' was the first rumour. Then confusion . . . One dead . . . Six dead . . . Twelve dead . . .

Parents raced to the school, passed by the ambulances taking away the wounded children to Stirling Royal Infirmary. Minds racing, eyes wide with panic, they arrived at the gates to find their entry barred by policemen.

They waited, huddled in disbelief and anguish, to find out whether their children were among the victims.

Eventually it emerged that the pupils who had lost their lives were in Primary One – the class taught by Gwen Mayor.

The parents of pupils in Mrs Mayor's class were separated from the crowd. Hours later, they were given the news that is every parent's nightmare, and it came with the force of a physical blow.

The heartbreak that followed was felt around the globe.

Seventeen coffins. The funerals. A river of tears. Precious memories. Unimaginable heartache. And incredible love and caring in a community that found undreamed-of reserves of strength and courage.

Dunblane, a Scottish town you would happily choose to bring up your children in, became the focus of world attention.

Prime Minister John Major, Labour leader Tony Blair, ministers and MPs from all parties, joined in expressing their horror at the massacre of the innocents.

Mr Major, who was in Egypt at an international terrorism conference when the news broke, said: 'My heart goes out to the parents, families and teachers of those who were killed and injured. No words can express the shock and the sorrow brought about by this mad and evil act.'

Tony Blair said the tragedy had 'devastated not just the tightly-knit community, but the whole nation. All our thoughts are with the families of those killed or injured in this incident.'

And the Queen, in a message to Michael Forsyth, the Secretary of State for Scotland, said: 'In asking you to pass my deepest and most heartfelt sympathy to the families of all those who were killed or injured, and to the injured themselves, I am sure I share in the grief and horror of the whole country.'

The world reacted swiftly. The area around the school was carpeted with flowers sent from all over the globe.

In the days following the tragedy the town was visited by Royals and politicians. Michael Forsyth, whose constituency includes Dunblane, was joined by his political rival George Robertson MP, who lives in the town and whose children once went to Dunblane Primary. The pair put politics aside for once and faced the tragedy in a united front.

John Major and Tony Blair visited the scene two days after the shootings and immediately pledged the money for the gym to be demolished and rebuilt.

It was the most poignant and testing of duties for the Prime Minister and the Labour leader. They were in Dunblane together. Two fathers.

Mr Major and Mr Blair emerged silent from the gym, pausing to comfort some young boys in the grounds by placing hands on shoulders. They toured Stirling Royal Infirmary where most of the injured children and staff were taken. They paid tribute to the medical staff.

A large number of the town's population prayed in a poignant service in Dunblane Cathedral. They all came on that Friday night – Church of Scotland worshippers, those who follow the Roman Catholic faith, members of the Free Church of Scotland, Episcopalians and Quakers. Eight clergymen from Dunblane's five denominations were on hand to lead prayers and offer pastoral help.

Two days later, the Queen and the Princess Royal visited Dunblane to pay their respects. The nation joined in a minute's silence. The Queen shed a tear as she talked at Dunblane Cathedral to mums and dads of the children who died. They also visited the injured at Stirling Royal Infirmary.

The next day – Monday, 18 March – came the first of the funerals. Joanna Ross and Emma Crozier, followed by Abigail McLennan and Kevin Hasell. Then David Kerr, Melissa Currie, Charlotte Dunn, Megan Turner, Sophie North and Hannah Scott. Little John Petrie,

Victoria Clydesdale, Emily Morton and Mhairi McBeath followed. Finally, on 21 March, Brett McKinnon, Ross Irvine and their beloved teacher Gwen Mayor.

The world cried with the people of Dunblane.

A corner of Dunblane cemetery was turned into a silent classroom where most of the tiny victims and their teacher lie at rest amid a sea of flowers, never to be forgotten.

On 22 March, Dunblane Primary School was reopened, except for the gym, which was demolished on 10 April.

People all over the world gave generously to help the shattered community. Millions of pounds were raised to help the families of the victims and to rebuild the social framework of the town.

Police announced a guns amnesty, and firearms were handed in to forces across the entire country.

Millions of people signed petitions calling for a total ban on handguns. The first such petition was organised by the *Sunday Mail* and signed by more than 400,000 people throughout the UK. A group of bereaved families flew to London to hand it over to the Government. A petition organised by the Snowdrop Campaign carried 700,000 signatures and was presented to the House of Commons in July.

On 29 May, an inquiry chaired by 60-year-old Lord William Douglas Cullen opened in the Albert Halls, Stirling. Victims' families attended most of the 26-day hearing. There were 171 witnesses and two tons of transcripts and submissions.

Among the harrowing stories, the hearing was told that in 1991 a policeman had warned senior colleagues that the gunman was 'unsavoury, unstable, deceitful and scheming', and that he should have his firearms certificate withdrawn immediately.

By this time the parents of most of the murdered children, along with their teacher's husband, had formed a close bond. They met every Thursday evening, supporting each other, sharing emotions. The families of the injured victims also met regularly.

With a united voice they took their plea for a total ban on handguns to the House of Commons. In October, the Government pledged to rid the country's streets of 160,000 high-powered handguns . . . but decided against banning .22 pistols. The decision provoked anger among the parents, who wanted nothing less than a total ban on all handguns.

One year on, Dunblane is battling through. Its heart is strong again, though it still aches.

The life of each of the 12 people whose stories are told in the following chapters has been touched by the tragedy in a different way . . .

A Mother – Kareen Turner relives the day that robbed her of Megan, the youngster voted in 1993 as having the happiest face in all Scotland.

A Father – Dr Mick North was coming to terms with the loss of his wife when he suffered a second tragedy – losing his darling little girl Sophie.

A Husband – Rod Mayor's teacher-wife Gwen died with 16 of her class. He talks of his pain, his pride and his plans.

A Teacher – Eileen Harrild, the gym teacher taking Gwen Mayor's Primary One class, who was horrifically injured.

A Shopkeeper – Irene Flaws, the town florist, worked round the clock to provide flowers for 17 funerals. Many of the victims had been in her Sunday school class.

A Campaigner – Pamela Ross, a grieving parent, was moved into the public spotlight in the quest for changes in the UK's gun laws.

A Politician – MP George Robertson, Shadow Scottish Secretary, lives near the school, and his children were once pupils there.

A TV Presenter – An assignment to cover the tragedy led Lorraine Kelly of GMTV and Talk Radio to a personal involvement with the families.

A Journalist – Newspaper columnist Melanie Reid was in Dunblane within hours of the tragedy. Her observations were highly acclaimed.

A Churchman – The Reverend Colin McIntosh, minister of Dunblane Cathedral, became a voice of reason amid the madness.

A Musician – Superstar singer Chris De Burgh offered his services on the day of the tragedy and became a friend and champion of the shattered town.

A Child – Coll Austin is one of the worst injured of the children who survived the hail of bullets.

This book has been written as a lasting tribute to those who lost their lives.

Victoria Clydesdale, *aged five*
Emma Crozier, *aged five*
Melissa Currie, *aged five*
Charlotte Dunn, *aged five*
Kevin Hasell, *aged five*
Ross Irvine, *aged five*
David Kerr, *aged five*
Mhairi MacBeath, *aged five*
Brett McKinnon, *aged six*
Abigail McLennan, *aged five*
Emily Morton, *aged five*
Sophie North, *aged five*
John Petrie, *aged five*
Joanna Ross, *aged five*
Hannah Scott, *aged five*
Megan Turner, *aged five*
Gwen Mayor, *aged 45*

It was written in honour of those children and staff who were injured.

Aimie Adam, *aged five*
Coll Austin, *aged six*
Matthew Birnie, *aged five*
Robbie Hurst, *aged five*
Amy Hutchison, *aged five*
Ryan Liddell, *aged five*
Mark Mullan, *aged five*
Andrew O'Donnell, *aged five*
Victoria Porteous, *aged five*
Robert Purves, *aged five*
Benjamin Vallance, *aged five*
Stewart Weir, *aged six*
Mary Blake
Eileen Harrild

But it has also been written with one conscious omission – the name of the coward who perpetrated one of the world's worst-ever mass murders. His name is not worthy of appearing in print alongside those men, women and children who were affected by his wanton destruction.

Quite simply he has no place in this story of courage and hope.

Peter Samson and Alan Crow,
March 1997

1. A MOTHER

HER bright, blue eyes mist over as she nervously fingers the gold oval-shaped locket hanging loosely around her neck. She stares out of the window, her gaze falling on the brightly coloured plastic kiddie's chute in the garden. She takes a deep breath.

Kareen Turner is talking about Megan, the little girl she lost. A grin plays around Kareen's lips as she remembers her daughter's mischievous smile . . . a dazzling stretch of a smile which had the ability to light up a room and which won her a national competition when she was only three.

'Megan lives in my heart now,' she whispers as she pulls again on the necklace containing her daughter's photograph. 'She lives in the hearts of everyone who knew her. Her smile touched so many people.'

Megan Turner was the five-year-old who loved nothing better than performing handstands and cartwheels, her pony-tail swinging from side to side as she went through her routine.

It is ironic that her life was cut short in a gym – her favourite place.

'She might have been a famous gymnast one day. Now we'll never know.'

A tiny, framed picture sits close by. Megan painted it herself. It's as precious to Kareen as life itself . . .

Megan's lust for adventure is captured perfectly in her carefree brush strokes. She painted it at Dunblane Primary School, a farewell gift for a trainee nursery nurse.

It's Megan's image of herself – a picture of an angel with blonde hair. Underneath is her name, written all by herself. She must have been so proud, sitting at her desk, carefully spelling out the letters m-e-g-a-n.

'When I think of Megan now I remember a bright, bubbly child full of energy. I remember her running down to the school bus. I remember her trying to put her roller-skates on. I remember all these things.

'Sometimes on a dark night I look up at the stars and I think: "That's all the children shining down on us." Or if I hear music, or some laughter I think: "That will be our children."

'And when I'm walking in the wind and the rain, I'll hear her voice. She'll never die because she is now with me. Inside me.'

Megan, a name which means 'great and mighty and a pearl'.

Kareen Turner clings desperately to her fond memories. Her story is one of love, heartbreak and bravery.

The morning of Wednesday, 13 March, was typical of most in the Turner household. Kareen and husband Willie were up first, anxious to get a head start before waking Megan and her little brother Duncan. They were both working that day. Kareen, a trainee nursery nurse, was starting a week's placement at Borestone Primary School in Stirling. Willie was getting ready for work at Kareen's dad's electrical business in Dunblane.

Breakfast television was babbling away in the living-room, but there wasn't time to watch it. Too much to do. Kareen began pouring out two bowls of cereal for the kids. It was 8 a.m. Time to get them up.

Megan jumped out of her top bunk, brushing aside the mini-mountain of teddies and soft toys. Her school clothes were on the radiator as usual. She loved to dress herself in the morning, although sometimes mum would give her a hand if she was a bit slow.

She pulled on her blue polo shirt, wriggled into her new grey pinafore with her cardigan on top, and put on a bright red pair of tights and a pair of Pocahontas socks. She bounded down the stairs for breakfast.

'I think we were running a bit late that morning,' recalled Kareen. 'We all had to be out of the door by 8.30 a.m. and it was a real rush to get Duncan ready to go next door to our childminder, Amanda.

'Mornings are usually pretty eventful in our house. There's always somebody moaning or chirping away about something or other.'

There was snow on the ground that day and it was pretty cold, so Megan put on her coat and her special Batman wellies before leaving the house.

'Megan got the bus to school and she would usually meet a couple of her pals outside the house and walk with them to the bottom of the road. That morning they came out of their front doors just as Megan was leaving.

'I remember shouting to her that she would have to hurry to catch the bus, as she was a little late leaving the house and she and her two friends were dawdling a bit going down the road.

'She'd been going to school on the bus since her second day there. On her first day I took her in the car, but on the second she was adamant she wanted to go in the bus, so I let her, but I followed in the car, parked near the school and spied on her just to make sure she was all right.

'Megan loved school, but it was always a big secret with her. You never really knew what was going on at school because she rarely told you. "We did nothing at school today," she'd say. She was in the second-top reading group and she had a new reading book home with her that week. I've still got it in a drawer somewhere.

'She loved drawing and colouring in. She was always drawing people. She would draw me, her dad and Duncan.'

Once Megan had got on the school bus, Willie left for work and Kareen ran next door to Amanda's with Duncan.

'I was due to start work at 9 a.m., so after I put Duncan next door, I drove to the school in Stirling. I was working with a Primary One class that morning, helping the teacher. I remember we were doing some printing work.

'I remember thinking there was something unusual going on because the teacher had left the classroom a couple of times. Around 11 a.m. the class teacher, Mrs Devine, came back into the classroom with the head teacher and they asked me to come with them. I remember thinking: "I've done something wrong. I must have made a mistake." Looking back now there was definitely something strange going on that morning because the school secretary had come in to sit with my class at one point, and that was very unusual. They'd obviously been trying to find out information all morning.

'They took me into the teachers' room and told me there had been a shooting at Dunblane and that it was a Primary One class that was involved, but they couldn't find out any other information. They said they thought it was a gym class and I was sure that Megan didn't have gym that day, but I couldn't remember.

'I went to the office to phone, but all the numbers to Dunblane were engaged. I remember what went through my mind when I realised that Megan may have been at gym. I just thought: "Oh my God, it will be Megan. She would be up there at the front. She would have been jumping about doing somersaults and cartwheels. She'd be in full view." One half of me was saying, "It's impossible, it can't be"; the other half realised she would be there doing her handstands and cartwheels out in the open. I just thought: "No, it can't be; no, it can't be." My head was spinning with all these thoughts and possibilities. It was a nightmare.'

Kareen dashed out to her car and decided to drive to nearby Bannockburn High School where her mum, Nancy McLaren, is a teacher.

'I don't know what made me go there, but I think I just needed my mum. I needed someone to help me. I went straight to the school office and asked for her, but she'd already left for Dunblane. She already knew. Whenever I drive that same stretch of road I still cry.

'It must have been around midday and as I drove to Dunblane I remember thinking that the roads were incredibly quiet. It should have been busy at that time of the day.

'It was strange, but I never thought to put the radio on. I was just intent on getting to Dunblane. I had to get to Megan.

'When I arrived in Dunblane, I jumped out of the car and asked the guy behind me: "Have you got a mobile phone? I have to phone. There's been a shooting in Dunblane." He said: "I know. Everybody knows." I just kept on thinking: "This is terrible. How could anything like this happen in Dunblane?"

'At that point I just knew there had been a shooting, but I didn't know there had been children injured or killed. Then I saw someone I knew and I shouted over to her and asked her what was happening. She shouted back: "It's okay. Megan's okay. It's Mrs Mayor's class."

'She thought Megan was in another class. She didn't know Megan was in Mrs Mayor's class.

'My heart just sank. My stomach was churning. It's hard to describe what was going through my head. I just couldn't take it in. It was just so unbelievable.

'Then I saw someone else I knew and I just screamed at her: "It's Megan's class. It's Megan's class."

'I drove on to get nearer the school. I stopped a policeman and said my daughter was in Mrs Mayor's class. He told me to get up to the school as quickly as possible on foot.'

When Kareen arrived at the school, Willie and her mum were already there. They were taken the short distance to the school staffroom, along with the other parents.

'The room was noisy, but it wasn't hysterical noise. It was incredibly calm. People were just trying to find out what was happening. My mum had heard that 12 children had been killed and others had been injured. She was saying this, but I wasn't really taking it in.

'It was like a bad dream. We just weren't getting any information and people were getting angrier and angrier. I just kept thinking: "Where's Megan? How is she? Is she hurt?" I just wanted to be with her. They kept us waiting for so long. All sorts of things were going through my mind. The ministers who were there just didn't know what to say to us.'

Then support teams comprising policemen and social workers took families away from the staffroom one by one to tell them the grim news.

'I find it hard to describe what it was like in that room waiting for your name to be called out. Not knowing what you were going to be told. Hoping for the best, but fearing the worst.

'When our name was called we were taken to the school music hut. The policewoman asked us to sit down. She held my hand and told me Megan had been killed.

'Strangely, I felt anger. I was angry that I'd been kept waiting for so long. I was furious that it had taken them hours to tell me my daughter had been murdered.

'I just wanted to see Megan. I wanted to be with her, wherever she was. If she was still in the gym, I wanted to be there. I just needed to be beside her.'

The distraught couple returned home to prepare themselves for the ordeal of formally identifying Megan's body in Stirling Royal Infirmary's Chapel of Rest.

'She looked as if she was sleeping. I touched her. She was cold. I didn't want her to be cold. I don't remember saying anything to her, but I probably did.

'It had been such a long, long day we just wanted to get back home

27

again. We were numb . . . so numb at everything that was going on round about. We just sat in the house, stunned. We had the news on and we found ourselves watching what had happened to US. We just couldn't believe it. Only hours earlier we had waved goodbye to Megan as she went for the school bus. Now it just didn't seem real. It felt like we were in a dream. How could this happen here? We could see pictures of Dunblane on the news, pictures of the school . . .

'But it did happen. We'd been to the school and we'd gone to identify our child, but it still didn't seem like it was really happening to us.'

Kareen and Willie had to try and be strong for little Duncan. And they had to tell the youngster that his big sister was dead.

'How do you tell a child something like that? It was a terrible thing to have to do. We just sat him down and told him that Megan wasn't coming home.

'Duncan misses Megan. He tells people he doesn't have a big sister any more. The other day he wanted to go to the shops and buy a new Megan . . .

'And if you ask him if he remembers what Megan was like he just says: "She was a great big star." It is difficult for him to grasp what death is all about. In the TV programmes he watches such as *Power Rangers,* the characters are dead one moment and alive the next, so he wonders why Megan can't be like that.

'Duncan was probably our saviour in the first few weeks, because we had to get up for him, we had to feed him and we had to look after him. It would have been so easy just to shut the curtains and not answer the door. He has kept us going. He still needs things done for him.'

The heartbroken couple had to start making arrangements for little Megan's funeral. It took place at Dunblane Cathedral on Tuesday, 19 March. Before the funeral, Kareen and Willie placed personal items beside Megan in her coffin.

'We took along a locket which I'd been given by my aunt a long time ago, a ring which belonged to my sister and Megan's "sooky", her comforter.

'I think seeing the coffin before the funeral made it easier than walking into the church and it just being there.

'I remember feeling that it was all so unfair. She didn't have a life to live. She was so young, they were all so young, even Mrs Mayor. I was angry that Megan was just a child and would never see anything of life. She wouldn't see sweet sixteen, she wouldn't have a 21st birthday, she wouldn't get married or have children of her own. She wouldn't become a famous gymnast. All that made me angry. I was angry because I wouldn't see her standing on her head like she used to do. I wouldn't see her doing cartwheels again. She wouldn't get the chance to be grown-up.'

As the couple are not religious they wanted a simple funeral for Megan – more of a tribute to their wee girl.

Kareen chose a song from her own childhood – 'Any Dream Will Do' from *Joseph and his Amazing Technicolor Dreamcoat*. Also, the theme from *The Lion King*, Megan's favourite Disney film.

'I said I didn't want hymns, and I couldn't make up my mind which song to have at the funeral. "Any Dream Will Do" came on the radio and I immediately thought: "That's it." When you think about it, the words are symbolic because our dreams were taken away. It's also a song from my past. I remember going to see *Joseph* when I was nine.

'I wanted something that everyone would be able to sing, and it's amazing, the song was sung with great voice during the service. We didn't tell anybody we had chosen that song, but everyone seemed to know it, even without words to read.

'It tears me to shreds whenever I hear it on the radio or the television now.

'Colin McIntosh, the minister at Dunblane Cathedral, was marvellous. I told him I didn't want someone standing up there saying "She's gone to a better place" or something like that. I wanted it kept simple, very plain. It had to be a tribute to Megan.'

The minister agreed to read a specially prepared tribute to the youngster during the service written by her grandmother Nancy.

'It was so beautiful. It just summed up Megan and her life with us. I had the words printed up and framed because I wanted to keep them for ever. They are so beautiful.'

Relatives and friends smiled through their tears as Colin McIntosh read Nancy's tribute to Megan:

> *Had we never loved sae kindly*
> *Had we never loved sae blindly*
> *We had ne'er been broken hearted*

They came no finer than Megan Turner. When we think of her we are uplifted, when we think of life without her we disintegrate.

At the age of 10 months Megan found her feet and from then on she used them to climb everything in sight.

We leapt to save her from the heights of window sills and backs of chairs, terrified that she would hurt herself. But as we realised that she had the flexibility and agility of a monkey, we sat back and relaxed a little.

By the age of four she quickly graduated to the big chute and spider frame in the Laighills – walking on her hands. We stopped worrying, recognising that her natural aptitude would keep her safe. It is ironic that when she was in her favourite class her life was ended through no fault of her own.

And then there was the other side of Megan – the artist. Many peaceful hours she spent drawing pictures – always for someone or other, and when colouring in she trained us well – 'Keep inside the lines, Granpa!'

Megan loved company and very early learned to adjust to the give-and-take needed in friendship. Her friends in her street will miss her greatly as they roller skate and cycle about.

Those class friends who are left will have their own memories but her love of them and her enthusiasm for Mrs Mayor was enormous.

To her brother Duncan and her cousin Fraser she was a friend, adjusting to their needs while protecting her own. We can think of no better memories than of Megan cuddling Duncan when he hurt himself or throwing her arms around Fraser when he came to play. She was the little woman in their lives and they will miss her greatly.

To her aunts and uncles and extended family she was very special as she included them in her loving embrace. Her horror of hair brushing disappeared for Aunty Avril and her forward rolls improved for Aunty Gail.

Her beaming smile and sparkling eyes captivated all who had the pleasure of her company.

To Grannies and Granpa, Megan gave five years of

undiluted love. She gave us so many reasons to live – and dreams were built around her – words are inadequate in attempting to show how much we loved her.

She was the wind beneath our wings. The phrase frequently used was 'I would die for her' – we weren't given that opportunity.

To her mum and dad, Megan was a joy, a burst of light, a wee girl full of vitality. They nourished her, encouraged her, protected her and loved her, bringing her up to be aware of the needs of others and showing her that love was the greatest gift of all.

Her smiles and laughter lit up their life but now that light has gone out. Their strength together over the last few days and their love for wee Duncan will carry them through.

We had only five years of Megan's life to hold and cherish. Our memories are brief but oh, how deep. Those of us who in some small way were touched by Megan must go forward and touch others with the same trust, respect and love in spite of the events of this week.

Her short life is preserved in our hearts, the pain of losing her is intense. We are angry that we didn't get much more of her but we will not tear ourselves apart longing for what we cannot have.

We will find the strength through the mutual support of family and friends to gratefully accept that we were privileged to hold her for five years and the memories will last forever.

'I was born and brought up in Dunblane and there were more than 1,000 people at the service. We were so overwhelmed by their presence and their cuddles. A collection raised £1,700 which was donated to Rachel House, the children's hospice in Fife.'

Little Megan is buried in Dunblane cemetery alongside many of her classmates and her teacher. Willie and Kareen visit her there most days.

'It's nice that they are all together there; it's such a beautiful place. Sometimes when I think of Megan I'll sort of whisper "Miss you," or if it's someone's birthday I'll tell her.'

Kareen wanted to visit the gym, the scene of the carnage, before it was demolished. She and Willie went there after attending Gwen Mayor's funeral.

'I did everything that I possibly could at that time, and I'm glad I did. I just felt I had to go to the gym, to see where it happened, where Megan spent her last moments. The gym had all been cleaned up, but before we went in a police lady said there was a flower where Megan's body was. It was strange going in there because I'd imagined there would just be one flower, but obviously other people had been in before me. But I knew where she was. She was in the centre. Most of the children had been together in the centre. I think I just needed to be where it happened. If in a few years' time someone asks: "Did you go to the gym?" and I hadn't, then I would have regretted it.'

When she thinks of her darling daughter now she thinks of the happy times. 'The memories will live on for ever,' says Kareen.

She remembers the little girl who loved singing and dancing.

'She would dance only when she was in the mood, but she loved country dancing. She and Duncan used to "hooch" round at my mum's, dancing to the radio on a Saturday night.

'Her favourite song was the "Spaghetti Hoop" song which Mrs Mayor had taught them. And she loved "We All Live in a Yellow Submarine". We used to get her version when we were in the car. All Megan could sing was the chorus over and over again. If we tried to sing the rest of the song, Megan would say, "Oh no, no, that's not how it goes." And so for 40 minutes we got "We all live in a yellow submarine" non-stop.

'She wasn't a material girl. You didn't have to spend money on her. She wasn't into the "in" thing. She never asked for the big things that some children get.

'If all she'd got for Christmas last year was her Barbie doll she would have been ecstatic. She didn't need anything else, she'd got her Barbie, that was it, no problem. We didn't bring her up to think: "I must have this, I must have that," and I'm happy that she was a contented wee girl. She didn't have to have everything. She appreciated what she got. She really appreciated life. It's a strange thing to say that a five-year-old could appreciate life, but she really could. She had all the opportunities that we could give her.'

Kareen and Willie were thrust into the public spotlight and the anti-gun campaign after the *Sunday Mail* carried a front-page picture of Megan, and launched a petition calling for the banning of all handguns. The picture of Megan, taken after she'd won a Happy Smile contest, touched the heart of a nation and became the catalyst for an amazing public response to the petition. More than 400,000 people signed up and pledged their support for a gun ban.

Coming only four days after Megan's death, the sight of their daughter's picture on the front page of a national newspaper gave them quite a shock.

'It really was quite a surprise. Willie came upstairs with the paper and said: "Where did they get that photograph from?" I remember thinking: "What right do they have to do this?" We were angry that no one had contacted us. But when we looked at it again we thought: "What are they trying to do here?" Then we calmed down and read it properly, and thought: "Oh well. Okay." It was then we realised the paper was trying to do something worthwhile, something positive. The paper was using Megan, using our daughter's picture, but it was to put across an important message.

'Later that week, we went into a jeweller's shop in Stirling and the petition was lying on the counter. I pointed to it and the assistant said: "Would you like to sign it?" I said: "It's our daughter," and she immediately took it off the counter. I said: "Oh no, please don't take it off the counter. Leave it there." Then she turned it over, and I said: "No, don't, just leave it as it is."

'It was quite amusing when I think of it now. The assistant obviously didn't think she was going to meet people like us, and the last thing she dreamt of was a bereaved parent, far less THE bereaved parent coming into the shop and saying: "That's my daughter." She just panicked.

'We're glad now that Megan's picture was used.

'She had a beautiful smile, but we never dreamt it would be used to start an anti-gun campaign.'

Later Kareen and Willie penned an emotional open letter to Lord Cullen, just before he was due to deliver his long-awaited report on the Dunblane tragedy. The letter appeared under a photograph of the couple tending Megan's grave. It read . . .

We write this letter to you with heavy hearts and anxious minds. If you've any doubts about recommending a total ban on handguns, take some time to visit Dunblane cemetery . . .

Wander round the walkways, look at the flowers and see the graves of so many of our little ones. Last week, we erected the headstone for our little girl Megan — a final act meaning so, so much.

When you're in the graveyard, spend a few quiet moments in the peaceful atmosphere.

REMEMBER how that atrocity in March shattered our lives, robbed us of our lovely innocent Megan, her fellow pupils and their caring teacher.

REMEMBER again how the Dunblane massacre shocked the whole world.

REFLECT on how these few horror-filled minutes changed so much for so many people.

We fully appreciate the huge task you're undertaking. No doubt you'll be crossing the ts and dotting the is in your report due out this month.

But please keep this thought at the forefront of your mind — the toll of human suffering should never be forgotten.

There are good days and bad days for us, but every day is filled with memories.

We think about what might have been . . . the children of Dunblane Primary School have just started back again for the new session.

The dead youngsters of Primary One should also have been starting again.

That morning was a hard one for us. Very hard.

That day was tough, knowing how excited Megan would have been, moving into a new class with a new teacher. She'd have been so proud of her new uniform and schoolbag filled with new pencil case and her jotters.

It's so hard not hearing her voice bubbling with the tales of the day's play, or lessons with Mrs Mayor.

It's even worse when we remember that one man's evil obsession with guns, and his wanton misuse of handguns, ended so many little dreams.

Over the past few weeks, the guns issue has never been far from the headlines.

At times we have sat back in bewilderment, puzzled at why people can even contemplate NOT banning handguns.

They're unnecessary, dangerous and sick symbols of society.

Remember the Sunday Mail *petition launched three days after the tragedy and which attracted more than 420,000 signatures, every single one demanding a ban on the private ownership of handguns.*

Some of us travelled to London to hand that petition over to Government ministers.

Our daughter's photo helped launch the petition into more than 850,000 homes all over the country.

Seeing her beautiful, smiling face beaming from the front page was tough. But we accepted we had to start getting the anti-gun message across.

We were shocked at the way some MPs failed to back a gun ban in the select committee report to the House of Commons.

Do these people have any compassion in their bodies at all?

We're worried your report falls short of our expectations.

Will your words be enough to convince the Government to introduce a law to ban handguns?

Lord Cullen, we make a last-minute plea to you – recommend a ban on handguns.

We want and need that. We urge you to do that. Our child, her classmates and their teacher must not have died in vain . . .

Kareen and Willie have found comfort in supporting the anti-gun campaign, but they've had to rely on the support of friends, family and especially the other bereaved parents to get through the last year.

'The support of the other parents is important for me. I need them. If I'm having a hellish day they know exactly what I'm going through, because they have had to cope themselves. They know what to say. They know how you feel. It's like a big roundabout which you are on. You get off some days and are able to do something else then you find yourself on it again, maybe having a terrible day. But we all know we've got each other and we've all been through exactly the same.

'I have moved on, but things are no easier. I'm worse now than say six months ago, I don't know why. I get very angry when people assume that because Megan died a year ago I've moved on. That isn't the case. It still feels like it happened yesterday. Something like this is still fresh in the memory. The kids at Dunblane Primary have gone back to school. They've had holidays and they've started a new school year. I still have great difficulty when the kids go back to school after a holiday.

'I sometimes wake up in the morning and immediately think: "I used to have two children, now I've only got one." When she was here I used to hear her jumping down from the top bunk and I would think: "That's her up now. Let's go." I miss hearing that noise now.

'I find myself rushing home to be with her for a certain time, forgetting she isn't coming home . . . People found it strange that I went back to college, but I'd nothing to be in the house for during the day. There was nothing there. If I stayed at home I would just cry all day.'

Of the locket she wears with Megan's picture in it, Kareen said:

'It's something tangible. I often find myself caressing it and touching it. She's in my heart. I can't see her. I can't feel her. I can't touch her. But if she's in my heart, she's there all the time.'

Kareen treasures a video filmed on Megan's last Christmas.

She only plucked up the courage to watch it just before the anniversary of the tragedy . . .

'I just sat and crumbled when I watched it for the first time.

'She was so excited, so happy. She's just got her Barbie for Christmas.

'But I needed to hear her voice again. People say that the voice is the first thing to go.

'You don't hear it any more. I needed to hear her.'

2. A FATHER

IT'S in his car that Mick North feels the hurt most. Sometimes he imagines he can hear her happy voice, sweet and gentle, like a song on the breeze. If he tries hard enough he can picture her smiling face; her tiny girlish frame sitting there beside him in the front. Just like she used to do. He can hear her scolding him for taking a wrong turning. Bossing him around. Just like she used to do.

Then, suddenly, the moment's gone, almost as quickly as it had come to him, and he is alone once more. Alone with his thoughts. Alone with his grief.

His darling, precious little Sophie died in the gym at Dunblane Primary School. She was the light of his life. His reason for living.

She was the girl who at the tender age of three, lost her mum, but still managed to keep his spirit and hope alive.

Perhaps she was too young to understand, but Sophie, the innocent girl with the bright, sparkling eyes, was somehow able to give her dad a fresh purpose in life and help him cope with his wife Barbara's death.

She was his companion. His little bit of Barbara still with him.

Now she is gone, too . . .

Where once there was a little girl's chatter, now there is only the sound of silence. Where once there was laughter and joy, now there is only death and solitude.

After Barbara died, Mick and Sophie did everything together.

They must have seemed an odd couple walking around Dunblane: the six feet two inch academic with greying hair and gentle, craggy face, and the mini-adult at his side, chattering away, keeping him right, her tiny hand pressed firmly into his.

She helped him meet people. She broke the ice when the shy biochemistry lecturer couldn't find the words. She was there for him . . .

A year after she was cruelly taken from him, his words hang heavy with sadness as he sits in the drawing-room of his pink-washed house in Dunblane. His gaze constantly flits on to his favourite picture of Sophie on the mantelpiece above the fire, her smile sending rays of warmth beaming down on his visitors, her cheeky expression still very much alive.

Sophie is all around that room. She's in the box of toys haphazardly stored in the corner. She's in the photographs which proudly hang from every wall. She's in the drawings she'd brought home from school. She's in the special poster with the 'I Love You Dad' message she made for Mick.

Mick North is already thinking about leaving Dunblane. 'It's not the comfortable place I thought it once was,' he sighs.

There were 17 tragedies in Dunblane on 13 March 1996. Perhaps Mick North's is the hardest to bear.

The town holds memories for him which are so painful, so hard for mere mortals to begin to comprehend.

Mick North had everything. A loving wife who shared his heart, his home and love of university life. Then there was Sophie, the little girl he'd always longed for.

Sophie was just a baby when Barbara fell ill with breast cancer. Despite a brave fight, the disease spread through her body and Mick nursed his wife through her final months.

When she passed away, Sophie was only just three.

'I try not to think about the unfairness of it all. That in losing Sophie, what I had left of Barbara was taken from me too.

'I don't dwell on it, but it doesn't seem fair . . .'

A noticeable spark enters Mick North's eyes as he recalls the happy times, the precious moments he enjoyed with the wide-eyed girl who made his life complete.

'I think that the photograph hanging above the fire sums her up. Smiling. Sparkling. I know parents can always be rather biased, but Sophie was just so bright. She'd catch on to things very quickly.

'She loved to talk. When we met people for the first time she could be a little shy for the first five minutes, but after that she always wanted to be part of everything. She wanted to join in on the conversation.

'She would always be asking questions. "Why this?" and "Why that?" she would ask.

'I think some of her "whys" were rather more difficult than questions asked by other kids of her age. I'm sure a lot of that was because the two of us spent so much time together, and I wasn't prepared just to talk child's talk all the time.

'I tried to make her interested in things, not by saying: "Look, that's interesting," but by talking about it a lot.

'It was especially true when the two of us were travelling abroad. There were so many things to look at. I would point out something that looked interesting to me, and she'd immediately pick up on it.

'I remember she once asked me why the moon changed shape. I couldn't fob her off with any old answer. I couldn't tell her the old story about animals biting a chunk out of it or something like that. Not Sophie; she wouldn't have accepted it. I had to tell her about the relative positions of the sun, the earth and the moon.

'She had a good attention span. She was bright.

'We had two trips to the States, which both lasted three weeks. It was mostly just the two of us travelling around, and I never felt: "Oh, this is a burden."

'She was like a mini-adult at times. It was a pleasure to be with her during these trips. She was a real companion, particularly when I felt she was old enough to move from the back of the car into the front seat next to me.

'It was easy to forget she was a child. Then suddenly she'd do something very babyish and she was a five-year-old again.

'I certainly feel, and have always felt, that Sophie helped me through the months and the years after Barbara died.

'It was inevitable that Sophie and I would become closer.

'I couldn't just sit around and be depressed all the time. I had to make sure Sophie's life was affected as little as possible by what happened.

'She was at an age that she was aware what was going on, but it is difficult to know exactly what she was thinking.

'Both the nursery and I tried to prepare her when it was inevitable Barbara was going to die.

'I don't know what her concept of death would have been at that age. The two of us were with Barbara when she died and it was something Sophie kept coming back to over the next two years.

'I don't think there was ever a time when Sophie didn't take it in her stride. That also helped me, because I never had to deal with a child who was reacting badly.'

Mick North clings desperately to the memory of his last morning with the daughter he treasured.

He awoke on Wednesday, 13 March, to find little Sophie cuddled-up beside him. She would often creep into his bed during the night, but this morning he'd felt her tiny warm body nestling in around 7 a.m. – half an hour before getting-up time.

'It's strange, but I clearly remember Sophie had cereal for breakfast, because for once she finished it all up and showed me her clean plate.

'There were often mornings when we were a bit grumpy with one another, as I wasn't particularly good at that time of day, especially if I had to get into work early, and she was slowing things down.

'But I remember that morning was more relaxed, partly because I had no lectures to give on Wednesdays, otherwise I would have been rushing in. Sophie was wearing her school uniform, a pinafore and a red sweatshirt.

'She was quite independent. Because it made things quicker, I'd often help her get dressed, but if she wanted to she could do it herself. The only thing she wasn't very good at was doing her shoelaces up, but that morning she wanted to wear boots, because it was very cold.'

His final memory of Sophie is of leaving her at her pre-school club, the Kids' Club, and saying goodbye.

It was just another morning.

'I drove her there. The Kids' Club is on between 8 a.m. and 9 a.m. and then again after school. These were the same hours covered by the nursery Sophie went to, so it was handy. It took a lot of pressure off me and I could work normal hours.

'That morning we left the house around 8.30 a.m. Normally we would have been away about twenty-past, but we had to scrape the ice off the car, so we didn't get to the school until about 8.35 a.m. I went straight into work from there.'

It was the last time she would sit chattering excitedly in his car. It was the last time he would see his darling Sophie alive.

Less than three hours later a knock on his office door at Stirling University would catapult Mick North into a world of horror, murder and pain – a world so alien to a man whose life had been dedicated to learning, to books and to academia.

'It would have been about 11.05 a.m. One of my colleagues came along to my office. He'd had a phone call from one of our students who'd been travelling to Glasgow for an interview. He'd been listening to the radio in his car. He'd phoned the university to say that he'd heard there had been a shooting incident at the school.

'It was difficult to believe, but then almost immediately two other people in the department, both of whom have children at the school, came and said: "Have you heard?" One of them was getting a lift to the school, so I went with him. I suppose I wasn't worried at first, because it could have been something minor, and we didn't have the radio on in the car to find out.

'I'm not sure when I actually knew what the scale of it was. It was obvious when we came off the bypass, and saw the roadblocks, that this was serious.'

Their car was stopped at a police roadblock, and Mick and his colleague were told to go to the nearby Westlands Hotel, where parents were gathering.

'We were given a cloakroom ticket when we went in, and I think mine was something like number 55. And they were calling out numbers and I think they got as far as number nine, obviously in an attempt to take details. I'd met up with Olwen Stacey, a friend of mine who had worked at Sophie's nursery and had looked after Sophie a lot while Barbara was ill.

'Probably no more than five minutes after that, somebody stood up. I don't remember whether he was in uniform or not, but he said: "This affects only one class. It's Mrs Mayor's class."

'And we were to go down to a house on the right-hand side of the school entrance. Olwen came with me, and when we got there quite a few other parents had already gathered.

'I think it was such a strange situation. I keep on thinking of how it is when you get awful feelings in the pit of your stomach. And I used to get those when Sophie would wake up in the middle of the night, worrying about her being ill. But it wasn't anything like that. It was so unreal.

'I went on to automatic pilot and said to myself: "I've got to go down to the house." And I just can't remember now whether I had gained any idea how many children were affected at that stage or not. Everybody was talking about there possibly being 12 victims.

'We walked down the road. The police didn't stop us. It just seemed very disorganised.

'It wasn't as if they were screening just those with children in Gwen Mayor's class. The entrance to the school was blocked with people. The Press were all on the other side of Doune Road, and I'm not sure whether the police were actually checking or doing anything to determine who were really parents, or relatives of the children in that class.

'And then we just stood around. The police wouldn't tell us anything.

'I don't remember a lot of talking going on. Thoughts were just churning in our heads. Olwen was still with me. I don't remember even talking to her all that much. I guess I was in there for about an hour. Then the police moved us into the school, in hospital patient transport vehicles, which was a farce. These things couldn't do a U-turn outside the house, so they had to be driven into a position right in front of all the Press cameras. Instead of shielding us from the Press, which is why these vehicles were used, the police set us up to be photographed.

'I would have been happier just to walk into the school.

'The tension was building up all the time. Then we were taken into the staffroom. Even by the time I got there some parents' names were being called out. The number of 12 victims was still the one that everybody had.

'Those of us that were left behind thought: "Well there have been about 12 families called out already, it's probably their children who have been killed."

'And then we just sat there. And we weren't told anything. The police kept saying: "We'll tell you something in three or four minutes."

'There wasn't a great deal of talking. I found myself just standing up, wandering around and just sitting back down again.

'Olwen stayed with me right up until the time I was told.

'I found the police behaviour at senior officer level was atrocious. It was as if we were an inconvenience. The idea to send in members of the school staff and the clergy and the doctors – some of whom apparently knew what had happened, knew our children were dead – with instructions not to tell us anything, was thoughtless in the extreme. I mean these poor people wandered among us rather like ghosts. They were laying their hands on our shoulders. We'd say, "Can you tell us anything?"; and they'd say, "No." So they couldn't give us any comfort because they couldn't tell us why we needed to be comforted. And I thought that was appalling.

'It was obvious that they knew a lot more. What we didn't know was whether they knew about individual children. I think it was awful, that they were made to go in beside us without being allowed to share what they knew with us.

'I suppose that I am not an optimistic enough person to have ever thought that Sophie was definitely alive. I always had a nagging doubt there. The situation was confusing, because at the time we didn't know who knew what. It was only subsequently that we found out that some of those with us had been in the gym, had seen the children and had been made by the police to keep it from us.

'I suppose among the thoughts that had gone through my head were: "What am I going to do if Sophie is permanently injured?" I mean there was time enough to think everything. I even thought: "Would it be worse if she were permanently injured rather than dead? No, of course it wouldn't. I want to have her alive."

'They were coming in and calling people out by family.

'I can't remember who did the calling out. They'd formed these support teams by then, and one of the support teams would call out the family names.

'Olwen and I were taken out by a social worker and a plain-clothed policeman and a uniformed policeman. We were taken to a school hut.

'And I suppose I still didn't really think: "Oh, this definitely means Sophie's dead," because we just didn't know how they were organising things.

'We got to the hut. It only took a few seconds. Then we sat down and the plain-clothed policeman started talking. It was clear they knew nothing about my family situation. I think he started off by saying:

"Mr and Mrs North." I stopped him straight away and said: "I'm a single parent, and this is my friend who has stayed with me."

'Then he went on and said: "You are no doubt aware there's been a shooting incident. Unfortunately 16 children have been killed."

'That was it. I knew immediately. He didn't have to say that Sophie had been killed. He just had to say 16. It was then we knew we'd got the numbers wrong, because there was no way that 16 other families had gone out earlier.

'It is very difficult to know exactly how I felt. For hours all these thoughts had been going round in my head: "She's dead, she's severely injured, she isn't injured." All these thoughts spinning round and suddenly finding that the roulette wheel has stopped on: "She's dead."

'I'd been having all these thoughts spinning round every three minutes over the last two hours and that's where it stopped.

'It didn't move on.

'I just felt numbness. I didn't know how to react.

'The first thing Olwen said was: "It can't happen to him. He's had to take too much already."

'The main thing I remember is going out into the playground outside the hut and someone said: "Can you hold on just another five minutes?"

'I shouted that I couldn't wait any longer. "I've been waiting for hours and then you tell me my daughter's dead. I want to go home now."

'It was just a momentary loss of temper. I think they said they would give me a lift by car, but the car never turned up. They were having all sorts of communications problems.

'So I went out of the back entrance to the school and there was just one person with a camera there, that surprised me.

'Returning home was very difficult. The day had been so long. The house seemed a different place from the one Sophie and I had left hours before.'

One of the heartbroken dad's biggest regrets is not knowing that Sophie's body had been lying in the gym most of the time he was anxiously waiting for information.

'Had I been offered the opportunity to see Sophie in the gym I am sure I would have accepted.

'I suppose at the time I thought that she would have been in hospital. And I now realise that her body was still lying in the gym all the time we were there. Again this is something that niggles me.

'I thought that everybody, whether alive or dead, would have been taken off to hospital within the first couple of hours.'

Later that night the distraught dad had to go through the ordeal of identifying Sophie's body in the Chapel of Rest at Stirling Royal Infirmary.

'I had to go and identify Sophie's body and that was awful.

'She looked younger and asleep. Not like the bright lively girl who had gone off in the morning, but more like Sophie two or three years earlier.

'I didn't say anything to her and I didn't touch her. I think I would have been allowed to, but I didn't want to.

'I don't know whether I had already made up my mind that I would want to see her again before the funeral, but I knew that there would be that opportunity, so that evening I had no urge to touch her.

'If somebody had said you should go and touch her, I probably would have done.

'That night I didn't sleep. I just kept waking up and shouting out.

'I imagined Sophie going to school. That first evening it was probably just seeing her face, not seeing her body, not seeing her as I saw her in the hospital.'

Mick spent the next few days being comforted by friends at his home in the heart of Dunblane . . .

But he had to come to terms with organising Sophie's funeral – less than three years after saying a final goodbye to Barbara.

He decided little Sophie would be cremated at Falkirk Crematorium as her mum had been. Sophie's ashes would later be interred in Dunblane cemetery beside her schoolchums and her teacher.

'I put myself first. I wanted privacy, I wanted it to be private. I am not religious, so there wasn't any local church I wanted. I decided on Falkirk, mostly because that's where Barbara's funeral was.'

Because he didn't attend any local church Mick decided against choosing a minister who didn't know Sophie to conduct the service.

But a minister, Ian Stirling, whose daughter Nicola used to go to nursery with Sophie before he moved to Ayr, volunteered to take the service.

'He was obviously the right man for the job. He was brilliant, because he knew Sophie from years before. His daughter knew her. So here was someone who did know her and had young children of his own and could understand.'

Then Mick had the task of choosing music for Sophie's funeral . . .

He wasn't keen just to have traditional hymns, so he spent hours listening to Sophie's Singing Kettle videos and tapes to find a song which he felt was right.

'I wanted a Singing Kettle song. I spent a lot of the evening before the funeral just going through all the Singing Kettle tapes, just to find something that would be appropriate, and I ended up with "Coulter's Candy".

'Later I wrote to the Singing Kettle, told them how important they'd been in Sophie's life, and I met them in July.

'She had seen them three times, twice at Stirling and once in Glasgow. And that morning, the morning of the 13th, I'd actually gone to buy tickets for their show. It was going to be in July, but I was buying them that far in advance because there was only one possible day we could have gone.

'They were important to her, because at around the time that Barbara died, she had begun to watch the videos at Olwen's house.

'After Barbara died I'd often say, "Oh, we'll put the Singing Kettle on"; and she'd sit and watch, singing those familiar songs.

'They seemed to me to be very much a part of Sophie's and my life, without Barbara.

'I just recorded the song and took it along to the funeral.'

Mick had taken Sophie with him in October 1995, to visit the place where he said goodbye to Barbara.

'Sophie and I had been to Falkirk on 8 October the previous year. That was the first time I had taken her there. I had gone back myself on the half-anniversary, and on the first anniversary of Barbara's death. In October '95 we'd gone over together and had a look at the Book of Remembrance.

'After Sophie's funeral I went back on 3 April, which is Barbara's birthday, because I felt Barbara had been somewhat forgotten. I went to Falkirk by train, so that it wouldn't be like going there for a funeral, and I spent some time wandering through the grounds.'

Mick North doesn't know how he has coped over the last year. He knows he misses his little companion. He knows she is all around his house. He knows his future is uncertain.

'I think there are lots of factors that are likely to have helped me. I think it would be too easy to drag myself down by saying this has been worse than what's happened to anybody else I know or anybody that I have heard about.

'I've just behaved as, and done what, I felt was right and I've not tried to manipulate what I do or how I feel in order to avoid this, although I don't pose myself questions to which the answers are too difficult. I did not want to find out too much initially about what was going on because I don't think I could have dealt with it at that time.

'If I'd sat around thinking, "Why me?" I'd not have been able to deal with that.

'That's not to say that there won't come a time in the future when I'm going to have questions. I'm only part-way down a very long road.

'There will be plenty of time to pose myself that sort of question, if I think I can handle it.

'I don't mind talking about Sophie, it does come naturally.

'She was the focus of my life and it would be impossible just to say, "Oh, that's it then," and forget about her and focus on something else.

'I live in the house where she lived all her life. She's all around in the house. There is no way of forgetting her and there wouldn't be even if I had to put all these photographs away.'

Mick has kept Sophie's bedroom as it was the morning she left for school for the last time. He can't bring himself to move any of her clothes or toys out.

'I don't go into her room very often. I don't sit in there for hours on end.

'But I did go and sleep in there, in her bed for a couple of nights either side of the funeral. I did that, because I felt that in all the rush of things that were happening before the funeral, somehow I had lost touch with her. And I just felt that I needed to do that.

'But I don't go in and sit in there.

'I don't know when I'll get around to sorting anything out in Sophie's room.

'I've got a great reluctance to throw anything out at all, and there's probably no need to. I could pass things on to other children, but at the moment I'd find it too difficult to be selective about it. Also I wouldn't know what in five or ten years' time I would have wanted to have kept of hers.

'There's no pressure on me, so why tidy it up?

'It's not being kept as a shrine, it's just that there's been no need to do anything with her room.'

But Mick believes Sophie lives on in the way she touched people with her infectious smile and bubbly personality.

'I believe that something lives on, but not in a form that someone religious would believe in. I think someone living on in your heart, is one way of describing it, but living on in happy memories is the best way I can think of, and knowing that I share these memories with a lot of people, who were influenced and affected by Sophie.

'People felt that she was special.'

Mick faces the future with uncertainty. He is considering leaving Dunblane.

'I still have to think my future through fully.

'I don't feel entirely comfortable here. There are some people who have tried to push themselves forward on the back of this image of the caring community.

'I wouldn't want to go simply because I want to get away from where Sophie was killed or where Sophie lived, but this is not the comfortable place I perhaps thought it was.

'I feel fairly vulnerable when I go out anywhere, but it often feels worse in Dunblane. I will sometimes go off to the supermarket in Stirling rather than go to Tesco just across the road.

'I could have decided not to get involved in campaigns, but I did get involved. I decided to write newspaper articles, which I didn't have to. But I think part of my vulnerability is simply because I miss my companion.

'I wouldn't be wandering around Dunblane on my own. As a single parent you can't go off on your own. Sophie would have always been with me, and as she was more outgoing than I was, she was the one who got me to talk to people when I probably wouldn't normally.

'So it's not just about this town and what's happened, it's also a reflection of my personality.

'I'm not the kind of person who just walks up to people and starts chatting to them. So I rarely find out if people actually know me or if they are just holding off because they are worried about how I am, or how they'll feel if I start talking.'

Mick visits Sophie's grave at Dunblane cemetery most days. He visited it three times on her birthday – 2 October.

'I just feel sadness. I sometimes worry that I haven't appeared to be more angry.

'I have this inner conflict going on all the time. Sometimes I really need people to talk to; sometimes I really need to be on my own. It's getting the balance right and being in control of what's going on. There've been a lot of mornings when I've woken up and thought: "I don't know what I am doing today."

'But I don't think I ever sat around brooding. I worked or did things at a much slower pace. So things that normally took a couple of hours seemed to take a whole day. I never felt as if I was sitting here and doing nothing.

'I carry a copy of Sophie's school photo in my wallet. I never carried one before.

'I had pictures of her in my office, but I'd never been one for carrying photographs around with me. A lot of the photographs were already in the house. I didn't suddenly change this and put up lots of photos that weren't here.'

There are times when Mick North sits alone at home and he thinks he can hear Sophie.

'Not so much now, but there were times when I'd hear noises. It was probably the cat, but I'd think that's her, what's she up to now?

'I don't feel that I should just be grateful for the five years I had with her, because I wanted 50 years.

'But there are a lot of happy, happy memories there that I can either think about myself or I can share with other people. That way Sophie can live on.'

3. A HUSBAND

ROD Mayor kissed his wife twice on Wednesday, 13 March 1996.

Once was early in the morning as she stood at the bottom of the stairs bidding him farewell as he headed off to work. Rod remembers that kiss fondly.

The second time was much later at night as Gwen lay dead in a hospital mortuary. Shot dead. Murdered as she supervised her infant class at school. Rod remembers that kiss too. And he wishes he didn't.

Rod entered the mortuary room on his own. He and his daughters Esther and Debbie had agreed that was best. Gwen's body had been prepared for the arrival of her next-of-kin. A patch was over one eye. A white sheet covered her body. Another was draped over her head like a nun's wimple. Her hair was not visible. Her still body lay behind a curtained, glass screen. Rod stood silently as the curtains were pulled apart. He asked the staff in the room if he could go around the screen towards his wife of almost 25 years.

'I kissed her. She was cold. It was such a stark confirmation of what had happened earlier that day,' he said.

Fifty-two-year-old Rod is sitting in the sun lounge of the family home. Patio windows look out on to a carefully tended garden, punctuated with rockeries, a pond and patches of lawn. Beyond the garden boundary lies a vast acreage of field and on the horizon proudly sits Stirling Castle. In estate agent's parlance it's a room with a view.

Gwen loved her garden, especially in the summer months. She'd drive home from school at lunch-times and sit on the patio in the sun, eating a sandwich, glancing at a magazine. She'd maybe manage only a half-hour or so but it allowed her an escape from the work environment and a chance to recharge the batteries. Her last pride and joy was a heather-filled rockery right in the middle of the garden.

Asked about Gwen, who was 45 when she died, and how the couple got on with each other, Rod took a deep breath and said: 'We never classed ourselves as being anything special. We just had a relationship in which we didn't argue about anything at all. I can't recollect having any real serious arguments. We never stopped speaking or that kind of thing. Possibly the only arguments we did have were over the children. But that's only normal.

'We always did things together when we could. We were members of a health club. Gwen would go after school and I'd often join her from work. She also loved aerobics and enjoyed keeping fit.

'Gwen had a flair about her. She could wear outrageous clothes for instance and look good in them. She had a couple of odd hats but she suited them. She was always very smart. She was stylish. She'd wear unusual ear-rings for the kids at school. She had a flair about the drawings and words she used in class. She wrote poetry although that was something we didn't know a great deal about until other teachers told us. They were like odes – nearly all funny about events and people.

'She had a distinct way about how she did her work at school. If I'd walked into Dunblane Primary School and looked around all the classrooms, I could tell you which was Gwen's class. I would recognise the posters Gwen had done.

'It's the same in the house. Visitors always said the place was beautiful, and that was all Gwen. The house is just Gwen. The furniture. The colours and the wallpaper. I would do the painting and woodwork or whatever. She did the rest, choosing the carpets and pictures.'

Gwen and Rod were due to celebrate their silver wedding anniversary in August 1996. They went out with each other for seven years before they married. Rod was 21 when he met Gwen. She was just 14 when they met in a youth club in Great Harwood in Lancashire.

'We didn't get married until Gwen was 21. She went to college in Nottingham and we'd decided not to get married until she had qualified. I worked for an engineering firm and we were supposed to be settling in Yorkshire, but I was transferred to Scotland to work at a power station in Fife.

'Gwen finished college in June and we were married in the August. When we came up to Scotland at first we had a rented flat in Stirling. Gwen hadn't been to Scotland before, and we agreed to come on the basis that if she didn't like it we'd go back to England.

'Because Gwen had qualified in England she needed to do two years' probation in Scotland. She managed to get a job at a primary school at Bothkennar near Airth. I could drop her off in the morning and, if I didn't work late, pick her up in the evenings. If I was working late, she had to get the bus home to Stirling.'

Later that year, the couple decided to buy a house of their own. They chose Bridge of Allan and plumped for a newly built estate. The house they selected was a three-bedroom bungalow. Their dream home. Rod admits money was tight when they first moved in.

'When we moved into the house we had nothing. The only pieces of furniture we owned were a coffee-table, a collapsable table and we brought a rented TV.

'We managed to buy a bed, a carpet for the bedroom, linoleum and washing-machine for the kitchen and a three-piece suite. When Gwen's parents came to visit we had to sleep on the floor. They gave us curtains and for months afterwards I used to pin them up on the piece of wood above the window. We couldn't afford the curtain rails. I suppose most people are like that in the early days. All the money we had went into the house.'

The couple had two daughters – Esther and Debbie.

It was in the last few years that the Mayors had seen their lifestyle changing. The girls were grown up, and money was less tight.

'When you've got a family you're committed to them. Once they move off you can do things you want more easily and possibly because you can afford to. We'd started going to the theatre together in Edinburgh and things like that. We were going out for meals more often – because we could afford to. We bought a caravan and started going away for weekends in it. We bought it primarily because for the previous 15 years we'd holidayed in France. First we went camping, then had our own tent and then a trailer tent. So the caravan was the next step. We used it to go to the Lake District where we spent a lot of time.

'Debbie was at university in London and we took the caravan down there. We went to a show nearly every night. We did feel things were changing. We had a bit more freedom, a bit more money to spend and we could look forward to planning different things.'

Rod remembers how committed his wife was to teaching and to her class of infants. She stayed on at school until 5 p.m. most days, preparing work for the following day's lessons. But, according to Rod, when she returned home the work went on.

'If Gwen was doing any special project then she'd work at home. On the dining-room table. And of course if there were 30 children in the class then it was 30 of this and 30 of that. She would spread the work out on the table. She always kept the place so tidy even at these times. She was just so particular.'

The couple had risen on the morning of 13 March at different times. Rod was leaving the house earlier than usual. He works as an area manager, covering Scotland, for an engineering firm. He had an appointment in Forfar that morning, some 40 or 50 minutes' drive away. Gwen got up to prepare for her day at work. Dressed and organised, she jumped into her sporty two-door Hyundai car – of which she was immensely proud – and drove the short journey from home to work at Dunblane Primary School. On the agenda that morning was school assembly, gym for her Primary One pupils and a meeting.

'We usually ran around in the house in the mornings, getting ready. I'd normally stand at the door and shout upstairs: "I'm away, I'll see you at . . . such and such a time."

'On that particular morning Gwen happened to be at the bottom of the stairs as I was going out, and we kissed. The significance of that kiss came a bit later, because when I found out about the incident, I don't know what it was – intuition or whatever – but I knew in my heart Gwen was involved.'

Rod's appointment with the client went according to his expectations. He sat back into his car, the next stop was to be Aberdeen. He noticed he had messages on his car phone. Two messages. One was from Esther. She sounded worried. In a panic. The other was from a friend, Arthur.

'Esther's message said there had been an emergency and to phone immediately. Then Arthur's message came on. He said something like: "I don't know where you are, mate – but for Christ's sake listen to the radio."

'And just as the message had finished and before I could pick the phone up, the phone rang; it was Debbie in London. She was hysterical, she was saying to me: "What's happening?"

'Of course I had to say, I don't know what's happening. She told me she'd been watching TV and a newsflash had interrupted the programme.

'And I said to her, don't be silly, things like that don't happen in Dunblane. She told me there had been an incident and that people had been killed. Debbie was becoming quite hysterical. I had to shout at her, tell her to put the phone down and stay by the phone until I could get some more information. I tried to phone Esther and got her answering-machine. I didn't know then but she was already on her way to the hospital.

'A short time later and Esther called and confirmed what Debbie had told me. She gave me a mobile phone number she was on. She also gave me the helpline number which the police had issued. I knew I had to return to Dunblane immediately.

'I drove back south. I managed to get through on the phone to the school. I expected to speak to the school secretary but it was a man's voice. I told him who I was and did he have any more information. He told me they weren't taking any calls on that number and all information was coming from the helpline. When I called there it was engaged. Constantly engaged. I was driving like a bat out of hell. I was switching calls – one to the school and then to the helpline. I needed to get more information, but the lines were engaged.

'Just before 12.30 I remembered that Radio One has its news slot at that time. I tuned in. As soon as they mentioned the incident it all fell into place. I just knew Gwen was involved. I don't know how or why but I did.

'Esther phoned me and I told her I had a funny feeling it's mum and that she should expect the worst. If we did that any other news could only be better. I was still driving. I got through to the school and I was beginning to wind up by this point. I said to the man who answered: "I'm Mr Mayor, I know there's been an incident and I know it's my wife's class."

'Again he referred me to the helpline number. "Okay," I said. "I'm coming to the school. Will I get access?" He told me I would.

'Strangely I was thinking, Why is he letting me into the school? The first reports said children had been killed. Then it said there were two adults dead.

'I arrived at the school just on 1 p.m. Police were directing traffic. People were milling around everywhere. I parked about 10 or 20 yards from the school. I walked into the school grounds. I saw people who I knew were parents of Gwen's pupils. I could tell from the look they gave me that it was Gwen's class.

'I said to a policeman: "I'm Mr Mayor – my wife's a teacher here."

'He went away and spoke to somebody else. I could see them speaking. They were looking down and talking. Then another policeman – a detective – arrived. He asked me to go with him. We entered the school and went into what I later discovered was the library. I told him I was virtually certain that my wife was involved in this incident. I said I've got two daughters: a 19-year-old in London, who is hysterical, who I haven't spoken to in over an hour; and I've got one down at Stirling Royal Infirmary. It's imperative that I know what's happened and I tell them. And I said, particularly my daughter in London because if she gets this via the media, I don't know what will happen to her. He told me that information was not available but that he would get back to me. I sat in that room on my own from just after 1 p.m. for almost 30 minutes. I kept saying five minutes more, I'll give them five minutes more. If nothing has happened, I'll do something.

'My mind was a blank. I just didn't know what to think. I couldn't understand why I was on my own and I tried to work out what I'd actually do if it was bad news. I could see people outside and there was a policeman standing by the door. I thought he was guarding me but he was covering up bullet holes. I gave myself a 1.30 p.m. deadline. Had nothing happened by that time, then I was moving out and getting the information myself. I had to know.

'At that time I went out and spoke to the policeman, said who I was and that I'd been left in this room since just after one o'clock on my own and I needed to know what the hell was going on. Because by this time, I assumed it had to be Gwen. I added that if I didn't get the information I would go out and speak to the media. The detective came back and I reiterated what I'd said. I asked: "Is it the worst scenario?"

'He still wouldn't tell me. I repeated I would have no problems in going out of the school and over to speak to the media. Finally he said: "In that case, Mr Mayor, it is the worst scenario."

'By that time the priority was to get to a phone to tell my daughters. I asked the policeman to take me to a phone. He said he was sorry, but there were no phones available. I said that wasn't a problem because I had my car phone. I'll go to my car, I said.

'The policeman said: "In that case, Mr Mayor, there is a telephone." To make matters worse it was in the library where I'd been sitting. I got very upset about that. They told me blatant lies. They knew immediately when I arrived at the school and could easily have told me.

'I picked up the phone, and believe it or not, dialled out and I got Debbie straightaway. I can't remember what I said to her. I don't really think I had to say anything. I think when she came on, I just said: "It's your mum." I can't actually remember. Debbie is adamant it was about ten past two when I called. I told her to stay put. She had a friend with her and the family she stayed with were there. I told her to sit tight and I would come back to her at some stage. I had to tell Esther. So I then tried to phone her mobile number. There were problems getting through. The mobile was switched off. The lines were engaged. Busy. It was just making me so frustrated.

'By then two people had come in. One was a lady called Helen Ruffell, who was introduced as a social worker, and a policeman called Scott Nelson. I was told that they had been allocated to me, or to us. Helen asked what the problem was and I explained how important it was to tell my other daughter what had happened. I said I thought she was in the hospital. Helen went off to try by other means. She had asked the hospital to put out calls on their Tannoy system. After the way I felt I'd been treated the arrival of Helen and Scott was like a burst of sanity. I actually started to feel something positive was being done.

'What we didn't know was that Esther had left the hospital and was actually in the school. In the same building as me. And she had been for over an hour. She had been put beside the other families. Suddenly Esther walked in through the door, into the library. It was then 2.45 p.m. We embraced. For a long, long time. I can't even remember if I said: "It's your mum." We'd all been due to go out for a meal the following day. It was Esther's 21st birthday on the 14th.

'We didn't stay much longer in the school. There was no point. We decided to go home. I drove home. The police wanted to drive me back but I wanted my car at home. I can't remember the actual journey back from Dunblane.

'We arrived home and the first thing we wanted to do was arrange for Debbie to come up from London. We knew we could get her on a train at tea-time but then it was decided to fly her up.

'We had others to think about as well. Gwen's sister was in Manchester. I called her home and got my niece who immediately said: "It's Auntie Gwen, isn't it?" Gwen's parents were away on holiday in Lancashire. We had to get to them – her dad was 83, and mum was 75. My parents are the same ages. We wanted to tell them before they heard it from the TV reports.

'It was arranged for Debbie to fly to Edinburgh on the 7 p.m. flight. The police had arranged for us to go to the hospital to identify Gwen's body. We decided there and then that we'd wait until Debbie arrived, so we could make a decision together on who would go with me. I went to the airport to meet Debbie off the plane. I still get emotional when I go to that airport now. Debbie was escorted from the plane first and obviously she was in quite a state as you can imagine. There were 150 or so other people on board and they were all talking about one thing and one thing only.

'When she came down the stairs in the arrivals lounge we didn't say anything. We just hugged. I don't think we said anything all the way back. The police had driven us and we sat in the back of the car and cried all the way back.

'We all left to drive to the hospital to identify Gwen just after 10 p.m. But there was some delay, and we didn't do that until midnight. It wasn't the hospital's fault. There were 16 other families doing the same thing. You can't rush someone in that situation. We were last to go in. We just had to wait. I had a chat with the girls, because all we had been told was that she had been shot. We hadn't been told how many times. So we made the decision that I would go in on my own first, because somebody had to identify the body. If I thought that she was presentable, they would have the opportunity of seeing her and they could either do that together, individually or I would go in with them. They had to make up their own minds. I think it's one of these things, that you only get one chance. If you don't take that chance you may live to regret your decision. We adopted the policy that we discussed things fully. If we didn't take the chance it would be lost for ever.

'I went in. We have never had a member of my family die before, so I didn't know what to expect. There were curtains over a glass screen. The curtains opened. Gwen was behind the glass panel. She was done up, almost like a nun in the sense that all you could see was her face. They had a sheet over her. And a patch over one eye. There seemed to be lots of people there. I asked if I could go behind the screen, and kiss her. They said yes. I think it was only then that I could accept it. Seeing her. When I kissed her she was cold.

'I felt that she was presentable. Obviously something had happened to Gwen's eye and there was a wound on the side of her neck. You couldn't see any of her hair. As I said, she was like a nun. I went out of the room and spoke to the girls.

'Debbie wanted to see her mum and went in on her own. She wanted to be on her own with her mum. Everyone else in that room left apart from one person. Esther wasn't keen at first. I suggested she go inside and be in the room. The curtains would be closed and once inside she could decide. No one would ask her what she did. If she saw her then she didn't have to say. In the end she said she did see her mum.'

After the hospital visit the family returned home. Debbie and her dad slept downstairs in the lounge. 'Debbie didn't want to be alone, and I really didn't want to be alone.'

Gwen's sister arrived from Manchester on the Friday. The two sets of grandparents came up on the Sunday. They were all brought up by the police.

'The death certificate had been released on the Friday afternoon, so we were able to arrange what we were going to do for Gwen. There was just so much to be done. I felt I had to be strong to get through it all for Gwen.

'We are not religious at all, but both sets of grandparents are very religious. Gwen and I had said a long time ago, that we didn't believe in graves or burial and that if anything happened to us, we had to be cremated. But then obviously, even in those two or three days it became clear that we would not be allowed to go and just have a private service. Something would have to be done that was not necessarily public, but would be for all the people that knew Gwen. We decided that there was only one obvious location for a service and that was Dunblane Cathedral. But there was the religious difficulty.

'The minister, Colin McIntosh, came to the house to discuss Gwen's funeral. I told him I felt hypocritical and yet I was asking to use the cathedral. Colin said it wouldn't have mattered which religion I was – the cathedral is a building for everyone. We decided to write a tribute to Gwen. Various friends offered to write pieces.

'I had only one request for the service. I wanted our special record played for Gwen. It was Whitney Houston singing "I Will Always Love You" from the movie *The Bodyguard*. Gwen and I had seen the movie. It sounds silly but we just liked it very much. If I put it on in the house, I would always say: "This is the song. I'm playing it for you."

'If I hear it on radio or TV, it hits me for six. The girls and I went on holiday to Cyprus and we were at the tour reps' night out. I got quite emotional before the end and fortunately I'd left and headed home. The last number they had played was our song.

'We'd sorted the cathedral arrangements but there was still the decision about who would read the tribute. We watched the Mother's Day service from the cathedral on the Sunday after Gwen died, and when I heard Colin McIntosh preach, I thought this is the man to read the tribute. He agreed, but then a friend, Arthur Gibbons, offered. Colin said he would step in if Arthur could not face it on the day. In the end Arthur read the tribute.'

On the day of the funeral the police delivered a trinket box containing the jewellery Gwen had been wearing when she was shot. A necklace she'd bought when Rod and she were on holiday in Tunisia was shattered. A bullet had left its horrific legacy.

'The girls wanted to wear something of their mum's at the funeral. Esther took a ring, and Debbie took a ring, and her sister took Gwen's watch.'

The hearse was piled high with floral tributes including the words 'Mum' spelled out in red and pink and 'Gwen' in cream flowers.

'The actual funeral service is a bit of a blank for me. The only thing that I can remember is arriving with Debbie on one arm, and Esther on the other. The door opened. Debbie went backwards. I had to pull her in. That's all I can remember.'

At the service Dunblane's assistant head teacher Stuart McCombie paid tribute to Gwen and told her pupils: 'Boys and girls, when you think of Mrs Mayor, be happy – don't be sad. Mrs Mayor will never forget any of you. Remember her lovely, smiling face and wonderful songs.

'Gwen has taught and enriched the lives of hundreds of pupils over the years. She had a lovely smiling face and sense of humour. Gwen had a gift with young children.'

The mourners heard him recount a story about how Gwen had organised a pyjama party for her class. All the pupils were excited. Except one little girl. Gwen tuned into this and spoke privately with her to pinpoint any problem. Asked if she was looking forward to the pyjama party, the little one burst into tears and said: 'But, Mrs Mayor, I won't be able to go. I don't have any pyjamas. I wear a nightie.'

Stuart added: 'They cuddled and the next day she went to the party with her special friend, a teddy, and with a nightie on and had a wonderful time.'

Colleagues at the school, according to Stuart, had smiled through their tears when they had talked about Gwen.

In his tribute Arthur Gibbons said: 'Gwen's qualities as a teacher extended beyond the boundaries of her professional role and touched upon her friends. Her final act was a positive caring one – she died caring for the young children who were placed in her charge.'

After the service the family had a private cremation in nearby Falkirk. Gwen's ashes are buried in the special section of Dunblane cemetery alongside 13 of her pupils.

Rod regularly visits the cemetery.

'I like to go as often as I can. There are not many days I miss. As I say I'm not religious and as far as I'm concerned Gwen's death endorsed my views that there isn't a God. Where the hell was he on 13 March? Was he on a tea break? I've heard lots of people saying he's done wonders since. He should've stopped what was happening then. I know the churches have been a great help to lots of people, and lots of members of my family, but for me, no. I think a lot of people must have questioned their faith after something like that. But I do get a great deal of comfort, satisfaction, from going to the cemetery.

'You'll always meet someone from the families up there. It's comforting to be there on your own. The first time I went there the place was filled with so many flowers the sight was absolutely incredible. There was just one huge mass of flowers.'

The response from people all over the world has stunned Rod and his family.

'But it all helps. It's just so emotional. We counted more than 2,000 cards and then we stopped. I think we got about 2,500 cards and letters in total. The three of us would sit down together and open and read them together. We were getting about 100 every day. We had a lot from people who knew Gwen, who'd worked with her over the years. And there were messages, lovely ones, from children who'd been in her classes. There was one from a little girl called Joan. I think she's six and a half years of age. She had asked for a photograph, and she had written the card herself. She said if we could give her a photograph, she'd put it in her best book alongside her hamster.'

Christmas and New Year were always going to be difficult times for the people of Dunblane. 'People said to me at the New Year, well you must have been glad to see the end of 1996, and you can look forward to 1997. I don't think 1996 has gone and for me, it will not have gone until the first anniversary has gone. Then a new year can begin.

'Wednesdays were never good days for quite a few months, but that has passed now.

'I'm not superstitious but you would be amazed at the number of times that 13 has cropped up. Apart from happening on the 13th, did you know the number of Gwen's classroom was 13? I only knew that when we went back to the school afterwards. A policeman let us into the school and we went upstairs to where Gwen's class was. They had forgotten to unlock the door so we had to stand there and wait. They'd taken Gwen's name off the door. I looked up and there above the door was the number 13. Dunblane's new school – where Gwen had applied for a transfer to – doesn't have a room numbered 13. It was a conscious decision.'

Several days after the tragedy Rod and his daughters made another visit to the school. This time they were asked if they wanted to see the gym before it was demolished. Again they agreed it was up to each individual if he or she wanted to go.

'We took flowers and the policeman on duty took a leaf from the bouquet and placed it on the floor to show where Gwen had been shot. The gym was the place where I had no real emotions. Other members of the family found the gym very difficult. But to me, for some reason in the gym – I felt nothing. On reflection it would have been nicer to light a candle on the spot where each of them died.'

Because Gwen had died while working, Scots law states that a Fatal Accident Inquiry must be held into the circumstances. It took place in November 1996 at Stirling Sheriff Court. Rod had decided that, as part of the families' campaign about the guns issue, details of her injuries should be made public. The Mayors would have liked to have kept these confidential but they felt it was the only way to highlight the damage a gun can cause.

Rod and his daughters and other Dunblane families sat in the court-room, reliving the horrors of 13 March. The Sheriff Principal, John Maguire, recorded that Gwen had been unlawfully killed. The two-hour hearing was told that six bullets hit Gwen. Her most serious injury was caused by a bullet which entered her right eye. It shattered her skull and caused extensive brain damage. It would have been instantly fatal. A second shot entered the back of her left shoulder, tore through her lungs and chest, out of her right armpit and into her upper right arm. A third hit her in the chest and came out of the side of her neck. A fourth entered her neck and went up into her mouth. Any of these last three bullets would also have been fatal. A fifth shot, which shattered her right lower arm before entering her left wrist, showed her arms had been crossed in front of her. A sixth hit her near the collar bone. She had tried to protect herself as the bullets flew. The Sheriff extended his sympathies to Gwen's family.

Rod has, in his own mind, visualised what happened on the morning in the gym hall. He's drawn some facts from the Cullen Inquiry and pieces of information from some involved. He's content with his picture of what he believes happened.

Rod said he and Gwen had discussed how either of them should cope if and when one partner died. 'We agreed that there had to be a positive look ahead, a way forward and that neither should reflect and dwell on the past all the time. I'm trying to do that. I find it hard to live in the house now that Gwen is no longer here. It's too difficult because there is so much of Gwen here. I've bought an old barn that will be renovated and eventually I'll move away from here into that. I'll never forget Gwen. I can't. I have too many happy, precious memories. My attitude is that we can't go back, we can only go forward. We've got lots of memories, and that is what we have to hang on to. We'd said to each other not to waste two or three years grieving. Remember the good times and get on. Having said that we didn't expect what happened to happen.'

Slowly Rod has donated most of Gwen's clothes to charity. Her evening dresses and special clothes have been kept. Rod has also kept the dress Gwen was wearing in the school photograph that was beamed all over the world at the time of the shootings.

The family has been involved in the setting up of the Gwen Mayor Appeal to benefit children in primary schools throughout Scotland. Its organisation is co-ordinated by the EIS, the Scottish teaching union, and Esther Mayor is a trustee of the charity. Contributions have come in from all over the world and the total has reached £50,000. The organisers hope to double that figure.

On 17 May Rod and his family will return to Dunblane Cathedral – this time for a happier occasion. Esther will marry her fiancé Mark.

'Weddings can be emotional at the best of times – but I think it will be even more so. We're beginning to think about the wedding a bit more now. These are positive things. Esther has bought a house and Debbie's looking for a flat. In that way they are becoming focused on the future rather than dwelling on what's happened.'

Remarkably Rod said that anger is the one emotion he doesn't have, following the massacre. 'I think it's because the man responsible has never been a piece of the equation. The best thing that could have happened was for him to shoot himself. So he's never really featured. We very seldom mention his name. As far as the other parents and we are concerned, we never think of 18 deaths, we always think of 17.

'I've had criticism that I haven't shown my grief about what happened. My grieving has been done privately. That first night I cried virtually the whole night. I just couldn't imagine what life was going to be like without Gwen. And then I got up that morning and I've got a 19-year-old to think about and another daughter who should have been celebrating her 21st that day. I had to be strong. There were a lot of decisions to be made.'

Rod admits he finds public recognition when he's out and about difficult to handle. He does concede, however, that he was behind the decision to take a public role in the anti-guns campaign. He doesn't regret that. Rod rubs his hands together and sighs heavily as he looks beyond the first anniversary and with determination reveals another of his personal decisions . . .

'When we get past the 13th of March this year, it is my intention to slip back into anonymity.'

4. A TEACHER

HER warm smile seems to embrace you as she walks into the room. Her bright eyes, full of life, twinkle down from her cheery face as she gently grips your hand.

Eileen Harrild's youthful looks belie her years. She exudes personality. She oozes charm. She radiates health.

To hundreds of tiny schoolchildren she was quite simply their gym teacher. They respected her. They trusted her. They loved her.

Eyes bulging with anticipation and excitement, they would race to be first into her gym. It was Mrs Harrild's class. It was fun.

A lot of the fun has now disappeared from Eileen Harrild's life. It was squeezed out of her suddenly one day by a madman with a gun. The smile is still there, the cheerfulness still apparent. But underneath the scars are deep.

Eileen Harrild's story is one of tragedy and incredible bravery. She tells it with difficulty, tears never far away from those bright eyes. The emotions are still too strong, the hurt too painful. But it is nothing short of a miracle that Eileen Harrild is alive today to tell it.

Eileen teaches gym in nine schools dotted all around Central Scotland. Her busy schedule meant that on Wednesday, 13 March, she was to be at Dunblane Primary School, which was also the school her two younger children Jennifer, aged 11, and nine-year-old Jack attended.

It was her second stint teaching at the primary school, having taught there in the '70s.

'Children were always coming up to me and saying: "You taught my mummy." That always made me feel absolutely ancient,' she joked.

Eileen was running a little late that morning.

She was due to take Primary One straight after assembly. On arriving, she began to set out the equipment for their gymnastics lesson. She could hear the children singing their hymns in the assembly hall as she walked to the top end of the gym and put out two sets of beams, which the children would use for balancing work, and two sets of ropes for swinging and climbing up.

'In the bottom part of the gym I'd put out some benches and there were hockey sticks which I used to make a shape on the floor which the children would have to tiptoe through. There were also mats laid out for them to practise their rolling.'

By 9.30 a.m., when assembly was due to finish, Eileen had all the equipment ready in the gym and was making final preparations as she waited for Mrs Mayor's Primary One class.

'I was ready for the class. I'd already nipped back to my room and got my file with the class list in it and the names of the various gym groups. I laid it out on a bench open at the right page.'

The first to arrive in the gym was Mary Blake, the supervisory assistant, who was due to help Gwen Mayor that morning.

'I was quite surprised to see Mary because she was normally with the Primary Seven class, but she said she had been helping Gwen.

'I knew the class had arrived when the first three children ran into the gym ahead of their classmates – they were obviously excited when they saw all the apparatus out and were eager to begin their lesson, having just spent the last half-hour sitting on their bottoms at assembly.

'The rest of the class came in. They already had their gym kit on, so I told them to start their warm-up. They began their stretching exercises, then they did some running. I told them to move around in spaces.

'I'd just told them to stop what they were doing, before I went on to the second part of the warm-up, when I was aware of the door being pushed open suddenly. It wasn't unusual for somebody to come into the gym to ask directions after parking in the car park close by.

'I was about two or three metres from the door. I immediately turned round because the door had been pushed open in such a sudden manner.

'I saw him very clearly. He was very close to me. He had a woolly hat, ear-muffs, glasses, a canvas khaki sleeveless tunic and a jumper.

'And he had his gun outstretched in his hand.'

For a few short seconds Eileen Harrild looked straight into the eyes of the gunman. She will never forget his icy stare.

'He had an expression of pure evil. Not madness. He had intent in his eyes. He knew exactly what he was doing. There was just badness in these eyes.'

Eileen didn't have a chance to say anything. The gunman pointed his pistol straight at her chest and fired.

'It was literally step, step, shoot. He only took two steps into the gym before he started.

'He shot me straight away, and instinctively I put my arms up in front of me to try and protect myself.

'It happened so quickly. I know it sounds incredible, but my initial reaction after the first bullet was fired was that this was a joke, an April Fool. A game.

'Then I realised there was blood pouring from me.

'The speed of the firing was so rapid and targeted that I felt that this man could only be going for me, but when I responded and instinctively raised my arms, I saw him turn his attention elsewhere, spraying everyone in his sights with bullets.'

The gunman shot Eileen four times – twice through the arms, once in the hand and once in the chest.

'By this time the children were screaming and running around in panic in all directions.

'As I turned, I saw him aim at Gwen and Mary. He went for the adults first because they were the only threat to him. Gwen had been sitting on the bench quite near me, having spoken to me when she first came into the gym. She'd put her diary on the bench and I had taken off a little boy's glasses and put them on top of the diary. Then he turned on the children.

'I turned away and staggered towards the storeroom. My glasses fell off as I stumbled, and I remember the thoughts going through my head: "This is unbelievable. What's happening? Why is this happening? Why is he doing this to us?"

'I reached the storeroom and slumped to the floor on my back. Somehow, Mary ended up lying beside me, to my right. She'd been shot in both legs and the head. Three children who had also been shot were lying at our feet, screaming. There were several other injured children lying on the floor at the entrance to the storeroom, quite close to us.

'The noise was deafening. The children beside us were screaming and crying, and the sound seemed to echo around the gym.

'I sensed within my heart that Gwen and some of the children were dead very quickly, because the shooting was so continuous and rapid.

'I realised we would have to stop the children screaming or he would know where we were, so Mary and I put our fingers to our lips and said "shush" to them.

'They immediately knew to be very quiet; very quickly they realised, they knew they had to stop screaming. As soon as we said "shush", "quiet", they lay down in silence. Not a sound. Not a whimper. It was very still.

'As they lay there one little boy whispered: "What a bad man, what a bad man."'

Eileen Harrild finds it difficult to describe the next few fear-filled minutes as she lay, helpless in the storeroom, waiting for the gunman to reappear at any second. Tears fill her eyes as she describes how she and Mary Blake tried desperately to think of ways of protecting themselves and the children.

'There was a pile of mats on my left-hand side, stacked quite high. I put my hand up to see if I could pull one down from the top. I thought if we could get the mats we could pull them over us, and perhaps he wouldn't see us if he came into the storeroom. I thought they would give us some form of protection. But, because I was lying on my back, I couldn't get the top mat to budge. It was a very heavy mat. There was also a huge rolled-up mattress which I thought we could use to hide one of the children; but it was at the far end of the storeroom, and I didn't want the children to get up and move and maybe attract his attention.

'So for the next two or three minutes we could do nothing but lie there on the floor just listening . . . and waiting. I was aware of him moving about in the gym. I knew where he was because of the noise, the terrible noise of gunshots. I could hear him walking around. The shooting was non-stop, continuous. Then I heard him opening the emergency exit at the top end of the gym. I knew the noise because it's a metal door and very noisy. I remember thinking: "Thank God. He's going away." The shooting was less rapid then. And then I heard him coming back into the gym. The next few moments, I don't know how long, seemed to last like an absolute eternity. It seemed to last for ever. We just lay there on the floor helpless, just waiting for him to come round the corner and finish us off. I find it difficult to explain the helpless and terrifying feeling of lying there waiting to be shot again.

'I wasn't feeling any pain. It was as if I was anaesthetised. All sorts of things were going through my mind. I remember thinking: "What can we do to save ourselves here? What can I do to save the children?" Abject terror. That's the only way I can describe it. The emotion of just lying there knowing you couldn't do anything. The feeling of disbelief that this was happening in our gym, to our children. It was just so unreal. We were so scared.

'We were all losing a lot of blood, but we were scared to move in case the movement attracted him and he came around the corner.'

As the pair lay with bleeding children beside them, waiting, fearing their final moments, Eileen turned to God to help her through the torment.

'It was just like the panic button had been pressed and I tuned in immediately to all these prayers, prayers I had learned as a child. I was saying them to myself.

'Then suddenly there was silence. Total silence. It was uncanny. There was no more screaming. There was no moaning. Nobody was moving, just an incredible silence.

'I just remember thinking: "Please God, it must be over now."'

Unknown to Eileen the gunman had turned his gun on himself.

'All of a sudden, help started to arrive in the main gym, and almost at the same time everyone started to react to their injuries.

'The children started to scream and cry and moan.

'Mary and I started speaking. She told me she'd been shot in the back of the head, and I said I'd been hit in the chest. I remember being really concerned that I had been shot there, more so than being hit in my arm and my hand. I remember there was an awful lot of blood; it seemed to be everywhere.

'I don't remember who was the first person round to the storeroom because there were a lot of people running around. But I remember Linda Stewart, a nursery nurse, helping us and telling us help would soon be with us. I remember asking her to get paper towels for the children, so they could press them on their wounds to try and stop the bleeding, and, rather oddly, also asking her to check that the ambulances would have easy access to the gym.'

As Eileen lay there, not knowing whether she would live or die, her thoughts then turned to her family – her husband Tony and children Anthony, Andrew, Jennifer and Jack.

'When Linda came over to me, I said to her: "I've been shot in the chest. I don't know if I'm going to make it."

'I remember giving her a farewell message for my family to tell them I loved them.

'But she was wonderful. She just looked at me and said: "Don't worry, tell them yourself!"

'It was a strange phenomenon lying there. At times I seemed to be quite coherent talking to Mary and the children who were beside us. At other times I can remember just calling out for help.

'By this time there were a lot of staff around. They were all trying to assist those who could be helped in any way they could.'

Eileen says she'll always remember the vision of headmaster Ron Taylor and assistant head Stuart McCombie coming into the storeroom.

'The expression on their faces summed up the horror of what they were looking at, and as Mary and I were obviously unaware of what they could see, it made us feel very frightened.

'Someone had forced open the storeroom doors to let the ambulances get at us, and I remember feeling very, very cold all of a sudden. I just started to shake uncontrollably all over. Someone covered us with football strips, but they were only made of nylon which didn't seem to help much.

'I kept shutting my eyes, trying to retain inner strength and energy because I didn't want to pass out. Mary and I were asking each other if we were all right. We were both bleeding a lot.

'The pain was beginning to hit me, and I was obviously in shock as my whole body was shaking out of control.

'Paramedics started to arrive. One came round to me and ripped off my T-shirt and began examining my chest wound. I was still freezing. I was just shaking and begging for help.

'Then doctors arrived. Two of them started to attend to Mary, and two to me. In all the chaos it was reassuring to recognise the familiar faces of two local doctors trying to put a drip into me. I have clear memories of Dr Herbert holding the saline bag as Dr Wright tried to put a line into my arm, with me tugging at his tie asking for help. My breathing was very shallow, and I kept shutting my eyes to try to keep calm, but was conscious that someone was trying to nip me to tell me to keep them open. I was only shutting my eyes to try to retain some inner energy, to try and be aware of my heartbeat, to concentrate on keeping it going. All the time I was trying desperately hard to control the shaking of my body. I felt very close to death.

'I had put my left hand over my right arm. There was a horrible, horrible big hole there. I tried to stop the blood, but when I took my hand off, it poured out like a fountain.

'I then remember looking at my hand. All I could see was a hole right through the knuckle of my ring finger. That was scary.

'The paramedics very carefully put Mary on to a stretcher because she'd been shot in the back of the head. They put a neck support on her to keep her head still, and it took some time for them to manoeuvre that on. They began moving the children from beside our feet, to get access for the stretchers which was tricky because it was a very narrow area with lots of equipment lying around. They eventually got a stretcher underneath Mary, and they covered her and put her into the ambulance. After she was inside they got me into the ambulance.'

Amid the mayhem, Eileen remembers her trip to hospital with amazing clarity – for one very unusual reason.

'Some of my senses seemed to have been heightened during the shooting and my sense of smell and hearing seemed incredibly strong. I remember hearing really clearly all the chaos that was going on, the talking and the shouting, the voices of the paramedics. It was all so incredibly noisy. I remember the ambulance man on the way to the hospital taking my mask off my face and slapping me. He kept slapping me. I could smell his fingers. They smelled strong. I could smell cigarettes from his fingers. The nicotine smell seemed overpowering. He kept slapping my face, and I kept on smelling his hand every time he did it. I thought I was going to be sick. I felt so nauseous, but I couldn't get the words out to tell him. I remember thinking: "Don't hit me. I've just been shot."

'I began to feel a bit warmer. I was shaking less. I'd been cold, so, so cold. I could hear the ambulance's sirens, and I remember thinking:

"It's not me. The sirens are not for me. It can't be me." When I see ambulances in the street I've always thought: "Oh that poor person. Oh God, I hope they're all right." But this time it was me lying there.

'When we got to the hospital, everything was amazingly efficient. They rushed us out of the ambulance into a room, and we were immediately surrounded by doctors. I lost Mary at that point; she seemed to be taken to another room.

'They started to take off my shoes, and they cut all my clothes off and they examined me very quickly. Then a doctor came to my side and whispered: "Your injuries are not life-threatening. You are going to live."

'I had an amazing surging feeling of relief. I can't explain the relief, the pendulum swung from not being sure if I was going to live to being told I was going to be all right and I was so thankful to be alive.

'I said to the doctor, "What about my chest wound?" and he explained that the bullet hadn't damaged any vital organs and that everything was going to be okay. I asked if I would lose my arm and he said they would do everything they could to save it. I just said "So be it." The possibility of losing an arm didn't seem like a big sacrifice. I was just so thankful.

'Then I was taken upstairs to another room. There were lots of nurses and doctors with me all the time. They were all marvellous.

'They started asking me questions about the type of gun which he used which I thought was strange at first, but they were asking me to help them so that they could treat the wounds of the injured children. I began describing the gun, telling them about the magazine underneath – anything I could remember. I really wanted to help them . . .

'But I felt I needed some answers too before they put me under the anaesthetic. I asked them how many were dead, and they gave me a rough idea how many children had been killed. I asked if Gwen was dead and they told me she was. It may sound callous and cold to some people but I really needed to know before they anaesthetised me. I needed to know.

'I was aware there were children in the medical bays near me. We were all waiting for the surgeons getting ready to operate. A doctor sat at my head the entire time. He asked me for phone numbers, so Tony could be contacted.'

When she came out of surgery Tony was waiting for her in post-theatre . . .

'I don't remember this, but Tony told me later, that as soon as I opened my eyes I shouted: "Did they get the bastard?" He just replied "Yes," and I said "Good" and then drifted back to sleep.

'I remember coming round to find both my arms were up in slings. My arms were covered in wire work and what looked like steel poles. Because all this equipment was on my arms they had to put my drips in my feet. I remember feeling like a dressed chicken.

'Tony came back to the hospital and I can remember being annoyed that he brought all of the children with him as I felt that the two youngest wouldn't like seeing me so soon after the shooting. Tony, however, felt that it was important for the whole family, although Jennifer and Jack did get upset and had to sit with the policeman outside the room for most of the visit.

'I'll never forget that first night, because I was so wide awake. The nurse sat with me, and I just broke my heart the whole night. I couldn't sleep. I was just so upset and I couldn't stop crying.'

Eileen underwent a number of major operations on her right arm over the next week, and initially only close family were allowed to visit her.

'I had no concept of the enormity of the whole thing. For some reason I just thought of this as something which had happened in Dunblane. I hadn't grasped the fact that this was having an impact worldwide.

'I was in this little room, and I didn't even know the man sitting outside was a policeman. I hadn't seen the newspapers. I hadn't listened to the radio, and I had no idea for that entire week of what was happening in the outside world. I was aware there was a memorial service on the Sunday morning and that it was on Mother's Day. I knew the funerals were going to start the next week and on which day each child's funeral was, because Tony was making arrangements to go to some of them. I was aware of what an impact the whole tragedy had on Dunblane and the local community because I was overwhelmed with cards and flowers. Then I began to get flowers and cards from abroad, and I think it was then I began to realise the full impact. I got flowers from people all over the world, from places like India and Australia. From people I didn't even know. It was a real comfort.'

In these early days in Stirling Royal, Eileen has sketchy recollections of being visited by the Queen, Prime Minister John Major and Labour leader Tony Blair.

'I don't think I fully appreciated who was coming to visit me. I knew they were coming, but I just remember thinking: "Oh that's nice, the Prime Minister's going to visit me." Other things seemed to be more important at the time.

'I remember Tony Blair coming in and standing at the bottom of the bed. He was very moved. I think he had just come up from the children's ward.

'He just said: "I don't know what to say to you." I thought: "How honest, that's okay. You don't have to say anything to me, it's nice that you're here."

'Then John Major came in, and I remember thinking how young he looked. Norma was with him and they were very relaxed with the family. I was really lifted by the visits.'

During the early days of her recovery Eileen found it helpful to talk about what had happened to her to both family and friends and also the medical staff who were treating her.

'My surgeon had to listen to it too. I talked, and talked, because it seemed so important for me to do that. It was part of a purging for me.'

A year on, Eileen is still battling back to health. She faces a nerve graft and further bone reconstruction.

'It is difficult at this stage to look into the future with any great certainty. As a PE teacher and someone who liked many sports, a lot will depend on how much use I will regain in my right arm. I'm hoping the nerve graft will bring back some more power, although after what happened, if I have to give up some old sports and learn new ones, then so be it.'

Now she's looking forward to the future with hope and anticipation . . .

'A lot has been said about the anti-handgun campaign which began here in Dunblane after the shootings. For me, as someone who has been directly affected by a legally-held handgun, I obviously have certain views, but importantly the strength of commitment from all the families and the Snowdrop Campaign has acted as a focus in bringing us all together with a common aim. When I think of all those beautiful children in the gym that day I still get incensed when certain politicians and members of the gun lobby keep telling us that it will never happen again and that .22 calibre guns are a safe sporting weapon.

'For the sake of all of us involved that day, I feel that I have to keep fighting to achieve something that whilst it won't bring back Gwen and the children, will at least help to make our society a lot safer – a complete ban on legally-held handguns.

'It's hard to describe sometimes, but perhaps the biggest influence on my life since March has been the bonds that have developed between Mary and me and the bereaved and injured families. We meet many of the families on a regular basis, and in a place as small as Dunblane we always seem to be bumping into each other. For a lot of the mums and dads it was initially difficult to discuss what had happened that day as Mary and I were the last adults to see their children alive. We are now very protective of each other's emotions, as only we who have been very close to this tragedy can begin to understand these feelings.

'All those involved now have a link that we know will be special for ever. We hope nobody ever has to experience anything like that again.'

Eileen Harrild only has to look at the scars on her arms and her chest to remind herself how lucky she is to be walking this earth.

'It's scary to think too deeply about it, because I would become paranoid.

'He thought he'd got me. I think he thought that he'd got everybody in the gym. He would have come back for us if he'd thought we were alive.

'I believe that before he shot himself he had a good look around, and there was nothing. No movement. No sound.

'He thought we were all dead.'

5. A SHOPKEEPER

ABIGAIL McLennan was in Irene Flaws' Sunday school class. On Sunday, 10 March 1996, she sat on Irene's knee in the church.

'She was one of these little girls who was bright and breezy. She had wee red shoes. You always saw the red shoes before you saw Abigail. I knew her mum and dad. I knew her mum from when I was at school.'

Five-year-old Abigail had a favourite hymn when she was at Irene's Sunday school at St Blane's Church in Dunblane. The hymn was 'He Took Me Up To His Banqueting House'. All the children enjoyed singing the rousing chorus.

Irene went to work later than normal on Wednesday, 13 March.

Dunblane's one and only florist loaded up her white van, reversed out of the drive of her family home and drove towards town.

In her rear-view mirror she could see children heading into the grounds of Dunblane Primary School. Her home sits less than 50 yards from one of the gates.

Minutes later she saw a face she recognised. It was John Petrie, aged five, on his way to school. On his way to Mrs Mayor's Primary One class. He pointed, waved and, as if telling her off, he shouted: 'You're late.'

Irene explained: 'I knew him all his short life. He was an only child and he was a premature baby. He was born just after my niece and I bought him a teddy the day he was born because of that. He would always say "Hiya". I thought he was a right old-fashioned boy. He was a right chirpy wee boy. He never walked past without saying hello or having a chat.'

A short time later and she saw five-year-old Joanna Ross walking to school with her grandfather, Jimmy. Irene remembers the bright pink anorak the little girl often wore.

Thirty-nine-year-old Irene could never have realised it then. She'd never see these three youngsters alive again. The next time she heard Abigail's favourite Sunday school song was at the little girl's funeral . . .

The week of 13 March was expected to be a busy one for the florist. Mother's Day was approaching and she had stocked up on pot plants for gifts and knew she'd need extra flowers to cope with the demand.

Wednesdays are usually half-day closing for Irene. If weddings, funerals or other special occasions meant more orders then Irene gave up her afternoon off and worked. That was just business. She's been running the shop in Dunblane's town centre for 20 years. She was used to hard work. Some mornings Irene was up at four thirty to drive to the flower market in Glasgow. On non-market days she normally left the house for the shop at either seven or seven thirty. The first customers would often find Irene ready for business well before her recognised 9 a.m. start to the day.

She looks back on the morning of 13 March. 'It was so cold that morning, I didn't leave home until half past eight. On Wednesdays I work in the shop on my own. I have a young Saturday girl and my mum and brother help out. My brother often does the market run.

'On that morning my mum was giving me a hand with the deliveries. I'd phoned my delivery driver and asked him to come over to the shop. They went off to do the orders at about 9.20 a.m. They delivered to the hospital in Stirling and I think we had one funeral that morning. Outside in the town it was just a normal Wednesday. Folk had dropped the kids off at school and at nine fifteen it starts to get busy.'

Apart from living in a neighbouring house, Irene had herself been a pupil at Dunblane Primary. She and her brother, Charles, were among the first pupils at the school.

The first indication for Irene that there was some sort of incident in or near the town was a rush of sounds.

'It was the noise, the sirens. It was about nine forty-five. I didn't really take notice of the first couple of sirens. Then they seemed to be continual. It was the intensity of it. The girl who owns the shop next door popped her head in the door and asked: "What's up?" I said I had not heard anything. My immediate thought was that there had been an accident, a crash, on the bypass. The roads were icy. That would be it. The school didn't even enter our minds. Why would it? Then the police helicopter arrived. We knew then that whatever was happening, it had to be serious. By that point we knew there was something very far wrong.

'The town actually went quiet then. It was so quiet. There was just this strange silence. I think there were traffic problems getting out of town. Then at ten o'clock someone came in and said there had been an accident. About 15 minutes later the phone rang. My brother was calling from Aberdeen. He'd heard something on the radio about Dunblane and an incident. I had my radio on in the shop, but the volume was turned down low. Charles just said: "What's wrong at Dunblane? There's something up but they don't know exactly what."

'Then about five minutes after that someone came in and said that there had been someone shot at the school. I was in shock then. I think I was just serving somebody, either that or I would have been sorting out the plants.

'I went next door to see Margaret in the shop. I asked if she'd heard anything going on at the school. She turned on the radio and at that point – it was one killed and others injured. There was a customer in her shop and she just let out a scream. It was obviously a pupil's mother. She wanted to go to the school, so she just ran but she left all her shopping, her handbag, everything.

'The chap who owns the fruit shop next door to me came in and asked me if we had heard anything, as he had two children at school. He went away and left his wife in the shop. I tried to keep an eye on her to see if she was okay. So then it just got worse and worse. Outside the town was just so silent. There was an eerie feeling.

'I turned up the radio then, but you were only getting little clips. We were standing around in disbelief, we just didn't know. We were told one child was killed, or one person was killed and then I just stood for a minute or two, and my brother actually phoned me; I then heard it was definitely Dunblane Primary School. No, that's not possible. The town that day just went like a ghost town. The only people you could see in the High Street were the police.

'By about 12.30, 1 o'clock-ish I decided to head home. The roads to the house were all sealed off by the police. I had to show identification before they allowed me through. As I came up the street there was only one person. That was our minister with his son who was in Primary Five at the school. He was just shaking his head. The minister had taken school assembly that morning. All he said was: "It's just unbelievable. I just can't believe it." You just saw the shock. He told me my brother-in-law Ian who teaches in the school was fine.

'Back at home we sat down to have lunch, but we couldn't eat. We switched on the TV to see the news. Outside at lunch-times the place is normally buzzing. Children would be moving around, and the playground lies right behind our house. The noise is always there. The school bell rings. There was no noise that day. The bell didn't ring that day.

'It never crossed my mind until the next morning, how crazy it would get. That first night my brother had offered to go to the market. I sat in the house and at one point was aware of a car leaving the school grounds. A couple were inside. I just knew they were parents. They'd probably just been told the news that their little one had died. I went back to the shop because I needed something for a wedding order I was working on at home. The place was swarming with reporters. At ten I went to bed but couldn't sleep. I just kept thinking about the horror of it all. Why? Why? Why? I felt so flat. I'd turned on the radio beside me because they said they would have a list of the murdered children. In the end I didn't actually hear the list because I must have nodded off. At about one in the morning I heard the list. It didn't sink in. I couldn't relate to any of them at all at that point. I got up at 5 a.m. and was in the shop an hour later.

'Streets were deserted. There was nobody about except some TV cameras and crews from the breakfast television news programmes. But they didn't bother us at all.

'My brother came in from the market. He brought a newspaper with him. The photograph of the class was on the front page. I scanned over it. Then I realised out of the 16 children who died, I knew 13. I also knew the teacher from delivering flowers to her.

'I knew some of them because I take the Sunday school class. I knew some through their mums and dads, because I had done their weddings, done their flowers when they were born. But Dunblane is not a huge place, you know, if the mums and dads come around the town you know the children. I am Dunblane born and bred as well.

'My thoughts when I saw it in black and white were, that I didn't want to read about it. I opened the paper, but I didn't want to read it. I didn't want it in black and white, I didn't want to read it at all.

'The first telephone call I had that morning was from the United States. It was from a man who comes to holiday in the area. He has a house here. He'd seen the TV reports of what was happening. He just wanted to speak to someone in Dunblane.

'We busied ourselves in the shop. Doing orders. Sorting out the materials I needed for the weddings planned for the next Saturday. Then there was a couple walked into the shop and he asked for a dozen red roses – he was one of the fathers of the dead children. At that time I didn't know who he was. It was just the tears. He said: "I want a dozen of your best red roses." I sort of swallowed, and thought what will I do here? My brother looked at me and I looked at him. We just gave the man a cuddle. That's all you could do. He wanted to write a card and I think he had about three attempts at writing it, before he could get what he wanted on it.

'And then about 8.30 a.m. my Saturday girl Fiona appeared at the door. At that time she was just 16. She should have been at school that day. But she said, "I thought you might need help." How a 16-year-old would cope, I didn't know; but she was brilliant. My sister-in-law came up to give me a hand.

'I think you go into automatic pilot, We didn't know how the day would go. And it just got busier and busier. There were people coming into the shop in tears. Most wanted a bunch of flowers for the school. The phone rang, rang, and rang. My sister-in-law's job was to answer it. Folk were phoning up and saying could we get some flowers and take them to the school. Victims' relatives were phoning up and saying would you take some flowers to my niece that I've lost. And it was the men with the hard hats and the big boots and the bunches of flowers in their hands. Off they'd go. To the school. That was what got to you.

'We were getting pestered left, right and centre by reporters and TV cameras. The BBC came in first. Their man Alan Mackay lives in Dunblane and buys his flowers in the shop. He asked me to do something on camera. I said I would.

'When people normally come into the shop they will chat away.

There was nothing like that then. It was the silence that morning that got to me.

'People who did speak just asked why. Why Dunblane? Why Dunblane Primary? Occasionally some asked if I knew the man responsible. I think I had come across him once in my life. But you know folk were just angered. Why didn't he just go out into a field and do it to himself and leave everybody alone? Or stand in the playground and do it and just shock the children?

'I was fine until one of the victim's grannies came in and then I just didn't know what to say to her at all. I had a visit from one of the local ministers checking we were all okay in the shop. He was going from shop to shop and seeing how all the shopkeepers were. It was just a mad day – all day. Folk were saying you're very busy and I would reply yes I don't want to be busy for this reason. I would have been busy for Mother's Day. I remember trying to take all the Mother's Day decorations out the window. All the posters. I just wanted them away. I had unfortunately left one chain along the back of the window, which I did not notice until the Saturday.

'On the Thursday we had phone calls from all our suppliers saying if we needed flowers to pick up the phone and they'd bring them. Other florists called to ask how we were coping and if they could help.

'At that point, we knew nothing about funerals, nothing about what was going to happen. Would it be one large funeral or 17 individual funerals?

'That night we delivered a vanload of flowers to the school. It was about 9 p.m. People were still milling around laying flowers. The road up to the school gates was carpeted with flowers. I thought there were a lot of flowers when I got there at that time, but it was nothing compared to the following nights.

'On the Friday people kept coming in to buy more flowers for the school. I thought we'd have to get stock organised for Mother's Day just in case. But in the two days, we added just two orders. Folk just were not thinking about that. By that point we had an idea when most of the funerals were scheduled.

'When we did, we knew we had at least six floral tributes for each one. There was a wreath from the primary school, one from Dunblane High School, a wreath from the Parent/Teachers Association, one from Dunblane Health Centre, a wreath from a local hotel and a wreath from the American gentleman who phoned that first morning. He wanted a wreath for every single funeral.

'One hotelier called us to order flowers and asked if we were coping and could he help us in any way. My brother jokingly said: "Yeah, eight o'clock tonight would you like to send down our dinner?"

'"Yes," the reply came. "And what would you like?"

'From that moment on we didn't have to think about finding anything to eat. He supplied us with dinner every night. We had to call and say how many people were working in the shop. Ten minutes later the food was delivered. We actually thought he would send down sandwiches. But that first night we got roast beef, the second night we got turkey and on the Saturday at lunch-time they sent down burgers and chips. People were so kind.

'Whenever parents or families came in we served them in the back shop. Then there would be a bit of privacy. It was hard. I coped with it by trying not to look at them straight in the eye.

'It was a case of a mum saying, "My son liked the Power Rangers." I'd say, "Do you want a Power Rangers wreath? I've never done one in my life, but we'll try one." If they wanted something we'd try it. But the worst task was writing the kids' names in flowers on wreaths. I found that difficult.

'On the Saturday night I took flowers to Dunblane Cathedral. I also had more for the school. By then there was just a massive sea of flowers. It was unbelievable. I came home that night. I sat down and I cried.

'A Sunday is normally my day off. I'd go to the church and take my Sunday school class. But that day I knew I had to work. My Saturday girl came in to help and members of the family came along for extra support. A minute's silence was to be observed. When the moment arrived we just stopped. My mother and I were the only two in the shop at the time, except for a reporter who had come in on the first day. He came in to observe the minute's silence with us. And we listened to the radio. There was a church service broadcast. I should really have been at church because I take Sunday school. But there was no Sunday school; it was cancelled. We started working about the shop, but it was a case of doing anything other than actually starting the funeral work.

'We started doing the wreaths about ten o'clock that morning, and it was 20 minutes past four the next morning before we got finished. The shopkeepers on either side of us gave us the keys of their shops, so that when we got a funeral ready we could store the flowers all together. We couldn't risk mixing up any of them.

'On that first night we made more than 200 wreaths. I did flowers for all 17 funerals and in total we made up almost 600 floral tributes in just over a week. That didn't include the flowers we did for the school.

'When I went to Abigail's funeral, the whole enormity of what happened really hit me hard. I had a half-hour to sit down. I settled into the church pew and the white coffin was right in front of me.'

Flowers lined the pavement outside the steep-roofed St Blane's Church. Little Abigail, who had two sisters, was described as a 'dainty little girl'. Around 300 mourners packed into the church. Dozens of townsfolk stood outside in silence.

'I just went to pieces. I was in a real mess. An undertaker who saw what was happening came over and asked if I wanted to leave the church. I had to pull myself together. I had to be there. We sang Abigail's favourite hymn. It was so difficult to believe what was happening.

'I returned to the shop and people were asking: "Are you okay?" I just replied: "Fine, fine, fine. Just let me get on." I knew we needed to concentrate on the next six funerals coming up. I didn't get home on Monday night at all. I worked right through the night to get the orders ready for Tuesday. I can go on for more than 24 hours at a time when I know work has to be done. I slow down and the work pace slows but soon the tiredness passes. We had to work that whole night. That night Ann, a florist from Motherwell, came to help out. When she arrived, we were frantically rushing around trying to track down a picture of Disney's Lion King. Someone had ordered a Lion King wreath. Eventually we tracked down a friend with the video and used that. Then we had to do a Mickey Mouse one. How many times do you see Mickey Mouse? But it was hard trying to visualise it for a wreath.

'I had a Power Rangers wreath on order and there was one I had a problem with. It was in the shape of a plate of Tunnock's tea cakes. The little boy called them Tea Pies. I found it hard. I shouldn't be having to do this. He should be eating his Tea Pies.

'Calls were coming in at an alarming rate. At one stage I simply had to unplug the phone for half an hour's rest. The telephone engineer appeared and said I had a faulty line. We plugged the phone back in. Calls came from all over the world – Sweden, Norway, Hong Kong, South China Seas and France. A lot of them had no connection to Dunblane at all. Some came from Aberfan. They got to me. They lost so many more children in that tragedy. The boys from the rugby club in Aberfan called to order flowers. You know, I can remember sitting in Dunblane Primary School as a pupil when the Aberfan disaster happened.

'One chap from Glasgow came through every day on the train and took a single flower up to every funeral. He didn't actually go to any of the children's funerals. He simply laid the flower outside. But he did want to go to Mrs Mayor's funeral. One family had driven up from Derby just to put flowers at the school. The four children had slept in the car overnight while Daddy drove up the road. People always asked for directions to the school.

'We should have had arrows pointing out the correct way to get there.

'I remember pensioners phoning up saying they'd put £5 in an envelope if we could put some flowers at the school.

'At one stage some of the children's families had 20 or 30 bouquets ready to be delivered in addition to the flowers they already had. Some had to borrow buckets from us to keep the flowers in the house. It seemed stupid sending up any more. I decided to draw up a list for each one. I called them and explained I had the list and that whenever they needed fresh flowers I'd deliver. One mother told me she had so many she had to hide some of them under the dining-room table!

'By the Thursday of the next week things had calmed down a bit. We had amassed so much rubbish we couldn't get rid of it quickly enough. We normally take it to the local tip but we didn't have the time. In the end I got a call from a friend who works for the local council. She had called to ask how things were. Was there anything she could do for me? "Yes," I said. "Speak to the right man to get someone to collect my rubbish."

'After all the funerals were over Dunblane started to change. No longer was it a black and white town. Colours started to appear. People out in the streets had changed their black funeral clothes for coloured clothes. There had been this sea of black. Everybody you saw was either going to or coming from a funeral.'

Twelve months on and Irene admits the tragedy has changed her life. She knows what happened on that blackest of days will remain etched in her mind for ever. She said: 'I live with the tragedy every single day. I see the school every single day. I reverse the van out of the drive and look to one side and I can see where the gym used to be. You can't get away from it. We've had 17 birthdays to cope with, sitting making up flowers for their birthdays thinking, they should be getting a toy or some other gift. You know this should not be happening.

'I can tell when the mums and dads are having a bad day. Because you get the silent treatment, when they are having a really bad day.

'We're hoping that once 13 March 1997 passes folk will leave us alone. We know they will never forget us . . .'

6. A CAMPAIGNER

PAM Ross was in her little girl's bedroom upstairs in the house. She spotted and picked up one of Joanna's shiny, black patent leather shoes that had been lying on the floor, almost under the bed. It looked grey. She ran her finger over the little shoe. It was covered in dust. Where she'd wiped her finger the black shone through. Pam didn't really want to clean it. The shoes were just as Joanna had left them before 13 March 1996.

She looks around the room. There are loads of tiny things like all these silly bits and pieces of paper you get from McDonald's. Stickers and labels. There are trinkets and toys and bits of plastic. A whole box full. Her 'jewellery' on top of the chest of drawers and clothes on a bean bag and chair. It's all too painful for Pam even to think about tidying them away.

Joanna had been excited about the arrival of her baby sister Alison. She wanted to call her Kate. She was glad when her mum and dad told her she had a little sister. Before the birth Pam and husband Kenny agreed that if the baby was a girl they would make Kate her middle name. They're glad they did. Now Alison, at times unsteady on her feet, looks towards the giant photograph portrait of her sister hanging by the window and points when her mum asks: 'Where's Joanna?'

Pam is determined that when Alison is old enough she will tell her all about her big sister. She'll tell her how she was a bright, happy girl who would spend hours drawing or watching a video, often on her own – content with her own company. Pam will tell how Joanna was great company, easy to talk to, and was logical in her outlook. She can tell Alison how much Joanna enjoyed school. She was curious and keen to learn. How she enjoyed staying at school for her lunch, one day a packed lunch, the next school dinners. How much she enjoyed being with her friends at school. She was always happy to be there . . .

'To look at Joanna she was neat, delicate and blonde and just very girlie. But she didn't particularly like dresses and once or twice it was a sheer fight to get her into one. She was very determined, at times thrawn, and she knew her own mind. But Joanna was also a charming and funny little girl. She was kind and affectionate – she would tell you she loved you, at times quite unexpectedly. She did have a favourite blue denim dress. I'd bought it for her and she loved it. In fact, when it was too small for her, she'd still wanted to wear it.'

Alison was just four months, still a babe in arms, when Joanna died.

'Shortly after Alison was born I remember saying to Kenny one night that we were so lucky. We've got everything we could ask for. We had two beautiful daughters. We just couldn't ask for anything more than that. No matter what happens now our life will never be complete because to me, at that point, with my two children, husband, home, everything that was comfortable, life was as perfect as I could ever have hoped for. Now that will never ever be complete.'

The telephone rang in the Ross household at around lunch-time, some four months after that dreadful day when Joanna, her classmates and teacher were murdered. It was a call from the lawyer's office representing all the bereaved families from the Dunblane tragedy.

The woman on the other end explained that a TV news programme wanted to speak to Pam. They'd asked Pam to call back . . .

Thirty-five-year-old bank worker Pam Ross was a grieving parent who emerged from the shadow of anonymity to become one of the campaigners of Dunblane. She never aspired to. She admits it was something she didn't really want to do. She didn't really believe she had whatever was necessary to do so. But in a space of less than 48 hours Pam had appeared on a live TV news programme and a letter she had written had been read by millions of readers in two national newspapers. Even now she looks back and questions how she summoned up the courage for it all.

'I don't know how I managed to do it. I suppose I did it for Joanna and all the other children and for their teacher Mrs Mayor. I suppose I just had to do something.'

Pam and husband Kenny and their families became involved in the gun campaigns launched in the wake of the tragedy. Pam backed Kenny and his parents, Jimmy and Betty, when they had travelled to London six weeks after the shootings to hand over a huge petition organised by the *Sunday Mail*. Pam stayed behind to look after Joanna's baby sister Alison. They also backed the Snowdrop Campaign which fought for a ban on private ownership of handguns in Great Britain. Then Pam and Kenny both travelled to London, meeting the Labour leader Tony Blair and Diana, Princess of Wales, at Kensington Palace.

They and other families joined the Snowdrop Campaign organisers in handing over the 750,000-signature petition to the House of Commons.

Pam reflects and admits it's hard to believe they were involved in such a high-profile campaign and met so many key people. She said: 'You expect to go through life not meeting anybody like that but you also go through life never expecting to experience something as awful as the shootings. These things all had to be done. A message had to be put across to everyone in the country and throughout the world.'

When Lord Cullen's inquiry into the shootings was drawing to a close at Stirling's Albert Halls, Pam joined the other families at a press conference organised by the families' legal team.

'Our main lawyer Peter Watson had suggested that we make some sort of public statement. Several weeks earlier a newspaper had asked the families how we were coping. At that point none of us really felt capable of being able to answer the question, because I don't think we knew within ourselves how we were coping.

'The reporter had printed out a letter with various questions on it, that being one of them, and I had sat with it one evening thinking, how do I really feel?

'Where do you begin to try and answer a question like that? I don't know how I'm coping. I thought, that is it really. We're not. We're still getting used to the reality of what happened on that day. We're devastated. I sat down and wrote down my thoughts and feelings. It was never used by the newspaper but I kept it.

'When it came to that press conference at the Albert Halls, the same question was asked and I had my notebook in my bag. When the question was posed, Kenny asked if I still had the words I'd written.

He nudged me and said that was the right reply. He said it did sum up how we were feeling.

'It was hard. We were all sitting along a table and when we walked into the room we were met with a sea of cameras and journalists. My heart and stomach were pounding, even before I knew I was going to say anything. It was the whole experience of sitting in front of the world's media. I was so nervous. I just kept my head down. I spoke to two of the other mothers who were beside me, but I didn't expect to say anything publicly at all. Questions were being asked generally, not to anyone specifically. Then, of course, Kenny prompted me. I panicked. I went into my bag and I took the note out. The reporters all waited with anticipation. What is she going to say? I said quietly "I've got this and well I'll just read it". I couldn't look at the cameras. I probably wouldn't have been able to say anything if it hadn't been written down. I came out shaking. What have I just done? I've spoken to the Press. Did I make sense?'

Sitting in her living-room Pam flicks through the black ring-binder folder and comes to the page.

'The question we'd been asked was about the courage and dignity we had shown and just really how we were beginning to cope. I said:

> *'The simple answer is that we are only beginning to learn to live with the reality of what has devastated our lives. Each day we live with the loss we have suffered and nothing in the future will ever allow us to feel that our lives are complete. There will never be a point where we can say we are coping and that everything is fine again, because it never will be. We will never get over it, we just need the strength to live with it for the rest of our lives.'*

Afterwards some sections of the media reported that one of the mothers had read out a prepared statement. But Pam smiles wryly.

'It was nothing like a prepared statement. It wasn't even intended for that purpose. That was the first time I'd really spoken to the media.'

She closed the folder, sipped from a mug of tea and said: 'I think basically that sums it up. The thing I feel really strongly about, then and now, is that nothing in the future can ever happen to us that could be as bad as losing a child in the way we have and that the impact of that loss will never lessen. Whether we have another six or a dozen children who would bring a lot of joy, or if we won the lottery or went on a world cruise. No matter how good these things were, from now on there's something missing. Still missing. Joanna's missing. I don't mean I can't see a way forward, but from here anything that happens will never ever compensate us for what we lost. Before 13 March, I thought my life with my family was complete. Our hope is that no one else will ever have to suffer a similar loss through the use of legally-held handguns.'

After that press conference a more nerve-wracking experience was still to come for Pam who works part-time for a bank. She returned that phone call from the TV news programme team in London.

'It was more out of curiosity I think than anything else. I didn't know what they were looking for. I didn't know why they wanted me or whether they were phoning round everybody asking for a response to some news item or other. When I got through they explained they wanted somebody to do the programme that night. It was live. There had been a leak about how the Home Affairs Select Committee would not back a total ban on handguns. They wanted a parent on the programme to give a reaction.

'I listened to what the programme reporter had to say. I hadn't said yes. I wasn't even saying maybe. Live television did not appeal to me at all. That first call came at around 1 p.m. It took until 7 p.m. before I was convinced that I could do it. That whole day was so full of tension. Was this what being a campaigner was like? Could I handle it? Did I need this sort of extra pressure?'

Pam had been invited to appear on the BBC's *Newsnight* programme. It's a flagship late-night, news and current affairs programme. One of its presenters, award-winning journalist Jeremy Paxman, is renowned for his fierce style of questioning.

'On that day I'd been contacted by Jim Cusick, a journalist on *The Independent* newspaper. He had chatted to me and I had agreed that an interview could form the basis of an open letter from me about the guns issue. I told Jim I'd been approached by *Newsnight* and he actually gave me a lot of help and encouragement although his article was totally separate. Talking it over with him helped me get my mind sorted out, deciding on the points I wanted to raise. He told me I sounded confident enough to him and that if I spoke in the same manner on TV I wouldn't have a problem. Easier said than done, I thought.

'I called back to the programme and talked it over more. Still I wasn't agreeing. Would I like to speak to Jeremy Paxman about it? He could run through what we'd speak about. I agreed. An hour or so later the famous Jeremy Paxman telephoned and ran through the various points he had in mind. "You'll be fine," he assured me. I wasn't totally convinced.

'I called other parents for their advice. I suppose I needed their reassurance that I was doing the right thing. I didn't eat the rest of the day, my stomach was in knots. I was so nervous, so uptight I couldn't eat, I just paced, walked around. I just couldn't do anything, I was so nervous – I couldn't sit down, drink a cup of tea, I couldn't do anything. I was just a nervous wreck. I spoke to Jim Cusick a few more times and I suppose in the end it was he who really convinced me I could do it. He certainly helped me take the final step to saying yes. Once I'd agreed to do it, that was it. It was all kind of frantic.

'The TV people organised a taxi to take me to their studios in Glasgow. Another mother, Karen Scott, offered to come to "hold my hand", because Kenny was working late. When we arrived in Glasgow the taxi-driver managed to get lost. Or at least he couldn't find where we were meant to be. He asked three or four people for directions. Don't do this to me. I'm on live TV in 20 minutes. We finally found the studio. I was taken into a small room and wired up. A monitor was on one side and I was told to look straight ahead at the camera. I didn't really want to look at it. I had no experience of anything like this. At work in the bank people are sent on training programmes which are often recorded on video, but I'd always avoided that.

'When I'd been speaking to various people I'd been taking down notes in my book. I decided I'd use them. I kept the book out of the view of the camera, but of course had to keep averting my eyes to see it.

'Suddenly I heard the title music and I could hear the rest of the people who were taking part. It all felt so unreal right up until the point when I heard my name and realised Jeremy Paxman was speaking to me. There was no going back.

'People have asked me if at that moment my words came naturally. They did – naturally from my notebook, at least for the first question which I'd more or less prepared for. The follow-up questions plunged me into further panic. Somehow words came out and I got through it. I remember being conscious of how many viewers would be watching – especially back in Dunblane. The families back in Dunblane were my main motivation. The whole experience was over in a few minutes but it seemed like an eternity.'

On the following day Pam made front-page news in *The Independent* newspaper with her open letter. And on the next day – after Pam had cleared the way – the *Sun* newspaper also ran the letter.

'I'd seen a copy of how the letter would appear in *The Independent* and I was quite happy. At that point I was aware of the fact that so many more people would be reading what I had to say. I think that was why I agreed. The two papers have entirely different readerships, so it was reaching different audiences.'

Pam's letter was intended to be an open letters to MPs considering the guns issue. Here is how it appeared in *The Independent.*

I wonder if you are all living in another world in Westminster, a safe cocoon where the real world no longer touches you.

So, today I'm going to ask you to try and imagine what you would feel if a gunman burst into the House of Commons and shot dead the Prime Minister and 16 MPs. Maybe you will say that nothing like that can ever happen to you. I thought that too. I thought these things happened somewhere else, to someone else.

But if what happened in Dunblane Primary School had happened in the House of Commons, would you all still be dragging your heels and trying to appease the gun lobby? I doubt it.

On 13 March I lost my daughter Joanna. She was nearly six years old.

Alison, the baby sister she had known for only four-and-a-half months, in a few years' time will have to start school. On that day, when Alison takes her seat in the Primary One classroom, I want all of you to come up here to Dunblane and explain to her the decision you have just taken.

Will you be able to guarantee her safety? Will you be able to tell her that another Dunblane could never happen? If there is no ban on guns, you will be able to offer Alison nothing.

I've listened to some of your attempts to justify this decision: 'It's not the guns that are to blame, it's people.' But I sat through the days of the Cullen inquiry and what came out was that there is no way you can decide on the suitability of someone to own guns. You can never foresee every circumstance they will find themselves in.

However, one clear fact is there to see – if guns were not legally available, such crimes could not be committed. If you do not understand this, then whatever reasoning you are using is flawed.

Over the weekend I went for a run in the car with my family. We pushed Alison in a buggy around the shores of a loch. My mind drifted back to the days when we did exactly the same things with Joanna, but she is no longer here and sometimes it feels like she's been wiped off the face of the earth.

I shared her life for five-and-a-half years, all her excitement and enthusiasm at school, all the promise she showed. I wondered if she would be happy, would she be a friend to her sister, would I be her good friend? All that has gone.

Now I have to explain to Alison why Joanna is not here any more. And I have to accept that Alison will never know Joanna.

You say people who shoot for sport would be disadvantaged if guns were banned. But do you value life less than sport? It worries me that you are accepting influence from the wrong places.

The police, who uphold and enforce the law, agree that guns should be banned. Yet, all of you seem to be ignoring this advice and instead accept the views of some fellow MPs and the influence of the gun lobby. Why?

Surely there comes a point when we all have to admit our society is no longer safe, and that to make it safer we should take guns away.

A RIVER OF TEARS . . .

THE CITY OF
DUNBLANE

HEARTACHE AND HURT . . . A policeman is overcome by grief on the darkest of days – 13 March, 1996. Hundreds of floral tributes were laid at the gates of Dunblane Primary School, the scene of the shootings.

FACING THE PRESS . . . The world's press descended on Dunblane on the day of the shootings. Within hours of the killings politicians and senior police officers faced a barrage of questions from journalists and photographers jostled for position during a press conference in the Victoria Halls.

BAN THE GUNS . . . Parents and relatives of the murdered children outside the House of Commons. They travelled to London to deliver the Sunday Mail petition, containing 428,279 names, to Home Secretary Michael Howard and Michael Forsyth, the Secretary of State for Scotland. The party also had a meeting with Prime Minister John Major.

UNITED IN TRAGEDY . . . Prime Minister John Major, accompanied by wife Norma, carries a floral tribute. They are followed by Labour leader Tony Blair and Michael Forsyth, Secretary of State for Scotland.

OUR SADNESS . . . Heartbroken Dunblane Primary School headteacher Ron Taylor, accompanied by some of his colleagues, walks to the school gates to lay bouquets in honour of the 16 youngsters and teacher Gwen Mayor.

ROYAL GRIEF . . . Her Majesty The Queen carries a single flower as she leaves Dunblane Cathedral. Prince Charles, deep in thought, is accompanied by the Rev. Colin McIntosh after the memorial service at the cathedral

THEIR FLAME LIVES ON . . . Musician and songwriter Chris de Burgh who has become a friend to the Dunblane families.

WORDS OF WOE . . . Newspaper columnist Melanie Reid was in Dunblane a short time after the shootings but said: 'I wanted to leave, to stop watching such unbearable grief.'

BOND OF FRIENDSHIP . . . GMTV and Talk Radio presenter Lorraine Kelly's assignment to cover the tragedy led to a lasting, close contact with the grieving parents and a special role in the national memorial service.

FLOWERS AMID THE TEARS . . .
Local florist Irene Flaws agonised as
she prepared floral tributes for the
victims. She knew 13 of the 16
children and several were in her
Sunday School class.

IN THE CORRIDORS OF
POWER . . . George Robertson,
Shadow Scottish Secretary and
Dunblane resident described
the speech he made to the
House of Commons on the
day after the shootings as the
hardest of his life.

A CAMPAIGNER

Listen to me. I and the other Dunblane families are not the first people on earth to lose their children through violent death. But our children were murdered. And all of you appear to be turning a deaf ear to everything that we are saying.

Pam emphasises that she played only one part in the whole campaign launched in the wake of the disaster.

'We all had our parts to play. There was a role for me, but I've not been the only one to do my bit. Each role has been different but each one was vital and just as important as the next. I have taken things as far as I felt able. Most of us had never been involved in any media or public activities before. We were not prepared for being thrust in the public arena – who would be after experiencing the loss of our children? Many of us doubted our own capabilities.

'We bounced ideas off each other and I, for one, always sought reassurance for whatever I was doing. I never went out on a limb and always needed the comfort of knowing that what I was involved in was right.

'Throughout the months after the shootings there has been a tremendous amount of teamwork among the group. I think that is one of the biggest factors in allowing us to achieve what we have achieved so far.

'A very positive relationship has developed between us and if you could say that anything good has come out of what happened it is the fact that we have made some wonderful friends, We share our feelings and spend time together socially as well as dealing with the demands in relation to campaigning.'

Pam cast her mind back to the day of 13 March – her last morning with Joanna.

She'd left for school with her grandfather Jimmy. He regularly walked with his beloved Joanna from her home to Dunblane Primary. Pam was back at home. She was on maternity leave from work, having recently given birth to baby Alison.

'I was having a lazy morning, sitting watching TV and giving Alison my attention. I remember thinking to myself how ridiculous this was, as it was late and I wasn't even dressed. The telephone rang and it was my brother Iain in Dundee. He'd been speaking to someone who'd heard a report about a shooting in Dunblane Primary School. That was at about 11.15 a.m. I'd only just come out of the shower and was up in the bedroom, just about to dry my hair. The first thing he said was: "Is Joanna all right?"

'I had to find out what was wrong and what had happened. Why did he ask me if Joanna was okay? I came downstairs and tried to phone the police or the school, but both were engaged. Then the phone rang again. It was Kenny's mum. She asked about Joanna. I got through to the local police station. The operator there told me there had been no fatalities. How could they be so wrong? She suggested I go to the school and collect my daughter. I tried to drive there but there was chaos. I dropped the car back home and started running to the school. On the road to the school I heard somebody shouting across the street that it was a Primary One class and that it was in the gym. I knew Joanna had gym and I just couldn't believe what was happening.

'There was a policeman at the gate and my neighbour who was with me pulled me to the policeman and said: "This lady has a wee girl in Primary One." I told him who the teacher was. Suddenly I was shown a different way from everyone else.

'I never thought about any children being injured, that's the weirdest thing. What if Joanna is part of it, what if we've lost her, what if she is dead? I do remember sitting thinking it is Joanna, she's dead, I know she's dead. But even then we didn't know how many dead. I was almost preparing myself for the worst. But I wasn't thinking of her being injured. All I could think was either she's dead or she's okay and if she is okay she would be screaming, she would be frantic, somewhere. I could visualise her and other children in a class or somewhere in a room, with a teacher, hysterical, wanting their mums. She'll be screaming, she'll be wanting her mummy and daddy and that's all I could think.

'It didn't occur to me that there would be any sort of in between, that there would be injuries, that children could be seriously hurt; and it didn't occur to me that she might be one of them, because I just didn't think of that possibility.'

Kenny and Pam were finally told the worst. Joanna was among the 16 children who had died. Pam struggles to recall the trauma of waiting to have the news confirmed by the police. She cannot forget being in that schoolroom with other parents waiting several hours before being called out one after another.

'We were second-last to be called. We realised that things were bleak. People came in and out of the room and they must have known what we were about to be told. The doctor sat holding my hand. I kept saying it didn't look good. Joanna's gone, she has to be. Why are we left?

'After being escorted to a separate room which seemed to take for ever, Ian Hamilton, the policeman, started telling us but was skirting around it. He mentioned there had been an incident. Joanna was in the class involved. Just tell us, we pleaded. Is she dead? Afterwards, having spoken to the social worker who had been assigned to us, we appreciate it was horrendous for them as well.'

Since Joanna's death Pam has written what she calls 'bits and pieces' about her little girl. 'I had problems trying to remember and visualise her in my mind. I'd look at a photograph and see her and remember from that. But I did have a problem visualising her in my mind, capturing a smile or mannerisms she had.

'We didn't have a video camera but friends do have little sections with Joanna at their children's birthday parties and I've seen these. I've been told to write down anything I do remember and keep it as a memory jolt. Whether we like it or not memories will fade, but the notes will help create a clearer picture.'

After they had identified Joanna at the hospital mortuary, Pam and Kenny asked if they could bring her home until her funeral.

'Her room was a real mess. It was just a tip, how she'd left it. Unfortunately the weekend or so before she'd been sick and it had gone everywhere. I'd had to clean the carpet and the bed. When we knew she was coming home we wanted to get the room back to how she would want it. Kenny tidied it up a bit. He didn't put things away as such but put toys in the cupboard and pens back in the tin. I made her bed up. I put her favourite Disney duvet cover on her bed and made sure it was made up properly. Joanna was then brought home and her coffin was laid on her bed. So we had her home from the Friday until the Sunday night. We got a great deal of comfort having her in the house for these two days.

'During that time we had a visit from Lorraine Kelly, the GMTV presenter. We'd watched her on the morning broadcast and had been impressed by her sensitivity. We asked our policeman Ian to make contact with GMTV to ask if we could speak to her. Surprisingly Lorraine made a special return trip to Dunblane and made a personal visit to us at home. That was the start of a special friendship that has since developed.'

Pam enjoys talking about Joanna. She describes her as 'a pleasure'. She recounts how Joanna had wanted her mum to find out about joining the Brownies. Pam had the telephone number but that call was never made. She remembers how Joanna loved swimming, having hours of fun in the water.

And Pam laughs loudly when she remembers Joanna dancing and singing to her favourite pop song.

'Since she had been quite small, Joanna loved "Relax" by Frankie Goes to Hollywood. It's probably something she shouldn't have been listening to but she'd dance on the bed to it. She liked it played on a tape in the car as well. The lyrics were "Relax, don't do it" but Joanna's version was "Lax, don't do ed" and that's what she called the song.

'Remembering her like that helps. Joanna was special to us all then. She is and always will be special for ever . . .'

Just the other day Pam had taken little Alison to the cemetery to visit Joanna's grave.

'I ended up in tears. There's a little ceramic dog on Abigail's grave next to Joanna's. Alison's been learning about the sounds animals make and she pointed to it, smiled and shouted "woof, woof". Then she ran around and played happily with the little toy windmill which had been placed on Joanna's grave.

'It broke my heart to see Alison laughing and playing at her sister's graveside. That's not how it should be. She should be playing with Joanna and sharing her laughter.'

7. A POLITICIAN

GEORGE Robertson knew it had to be something important. He had been embroiled in the middle of a crucial meeting in a room in the shadow of the House of Commons and surrounded by fellow MPs, when his buzzing pager gave him the first indication of trouble.

He reluctantly interrupted the Labour front-bench Scottish team's meeting and lifted a phone in the corridor. He called his office.

He was told that there were details coming in on the news wires of an incident in a Dunblane school and possible deaths.

These few words were to change George Robertson MP – for life.

Though he stood in the heart of British political life, his first thoughts were those of a dad . . . His daughter was a pupil at Dunblane High School.

He broke the news to the others at the meeting. They were all staggered.

'I said I was going home to Dunblane. Then I just took off.'

He raced downstairs to his office and immediately tried to phone his wife, Sandra, but the phone lines were blocked. But he did manage to phone Dunblane High School.

'I told them who I was and I asked them if everything was all right.

'They said there was nothing wrong at the High School, but they were hearing stories that something had happened at Dunblane Primary.

'I felt a momentary relief that my daughter was safe, and then another feeling – a sense of horror that how on earth could there be something happening at the primary school?

'My first reaction was as a father. When I heard it wasn't the High School there was a surge of emotion from knowing I was sort of in the clear. That feeling must have been paralleled in Dunblane when you think about the number of people who have kids at all the schools in the town. The instinct is to think: "Is it our kids?"

'To want to know that your own child is safe in circumstances where others have been affected is the first human, natural reaction. It's immediately followed by perhaps a sense of guilt, but also just a sense of hopelessness and horror and disbelief.

'There was just a feeling of "this can't really have happened. This is a town where nothing happens." This might be an aberration, a dream or something you had imagined. It was just the sheer shock of it all.'

George's pain had a strong personal element. He had lived in Dunblane for 20 years. His children had attended Dunblane Primary School. Although he spent a great deal of his time away from home because of his duties as Shadow Secretary of State for Scotland, he and his family are known in the cathedral city. He is well respected.

He recalled trying to phone home to his wife. All the phone lines were blocked. He needed to speak with her.

George Robertson is not a man given to easy emotions. The next few days would be filled with pain, heartache and tears. But the resolve and determination he had cultivated as a hardened politician were to stand him in good stead for the sheer horror which lay ahead.

'I just wanted to get back up to Scotland, to Dunblane,' he recalled.

'I was about to make travel plans when I got a message that Scottish Secretary Michael Forsyth's office was on the phone. They told me that Mr Forsyth was going up to Scotland immediately and they asked if I'd like to join him. I just said yes, absolutely.

'I tracked down they were going to be leaving from the House of Commons members' entrance. I was quite a distance away from there, so I came down the stairs and spotted a Labour Party van outside. It's funny how these small details stick in your mind. I was about to run to the members' entrance, which would have taken me about eight minutes, when the driver said: "Get in the van." I jumped in, but the van got stuck in traffic, even in that short distance. I got out of the van and I started to race along to the members' entrance. All I'd had time to grab were some papers which I'd put in a folder and my mobile phone.

'I got over to the members' entrance and Michael Forsyth was there in his car, and he was obviously able to tell me more.

'He confirmed that it was Dunblane Primary School. He said that a man had come into the school and a number of children had been killed. At that time they were talking about eight or nine dead and others injured. It looked pretty grim.'

Michael Forsyth, the Scottish Secretary and MP for Dunblane, and George Robertson, his shadow on the Labour bench, had never been what one would describe as close. Both men maintained the courtesies demanded inside the House of Commons, the pleasantries expected in a chamber famous for its pomp and ceremony. But there was always an 'icy' edge to the relationship between these two bitter political rivals.

Yet they found themselves sitting in the same car . . . brought together by an evil act 400 miles away.

'It was a strange situation. It was the Wednesday after the Labour Party Conference, which had been a fairly robust affair. And it was the Wednesday before the Scottish Grand Committee was due to meet in Glasgow. John Major was coming up for that, so it was a pretty excitable political atmosphere that week. I had launched a fairly tough attack on Michael Forsyth at the party conference, which it transpired later on that he had been reading. We'd been psyching ourselves up for the Friday, when there was going to be a huge demonstration in Glasgow against John Major. In the middle of all that we were suddenly put together.

'We were both pretty shocked. Something dire had obviously happened.

'The political animosity had gone, and we were basically two fathers. We were two political opponents, but that was just dropped.

'Another important aspect is that he had to go back. He is the Secretary of State for Scotland, in charge of the police and the education service, so he had an obligation to go. He is also the local MP. But he didn't need to call me either as his political opposite number or as a resident of Dunblane. So it was an act of selfless generosity which I think is something to his eternal credit.

'When the Lockerbie disaster happened the then Scottish Secretary, Malcolm Rifkind, took his opposite number, Donald Dewar, up to Scotland with him because there was an element of solidarity there. But I think in this case it was an instinct Michael Forsyth had. Whatever differences we have, and they are huge, in the political sense, I'll never forget what he did. From then on we were together. It was a pretty grim coincidence when you come to think of it, in a way, that this happens in a very small town in Scotland, where I happen to live and which he happens to represent.'

The pair, travelling with Mr Forsyth's private secretary, Michael Lugton, arrived at Heathrow and headed straight for the executive departure lounge to wait to board the 12.15 p.m. shuttle to Glasgow.

'The news came on the lounge television and everyone started watching. A lot of these people were learning for the first time that something had happened. They were all crowded round this television shaking their heads. A shock wave was going round the country at that point.'

But there was an even greater horror awaiting the two MPs as they took their seats for the flight north.

'Michael Lugton was passing messages to Michael Forsyth the whole way up. Mr Forsyth had this notebook that had been passed to him. He said: "I'm going to tell you something in absolute confidence. They think they know the name of the person who did this, and it's going to come as a bit of a shock to you." And he just opened the notebook and that man's name was written down on the sheet of paper. That name meant an awful lot to both of us. We'd both met him before.

'I don't even want to say his name, because that's what he wanted. I don't see why we should fall into his game. The whole thing was planned as a method of getting revenge, ending his own life and being remembered for it.'

But George Robertson had to put aside his own emotions and steel himself for the terrible task ahead – meeting people in Dunblane.

'We arrived at Glasgow Airport. There were some reporters there but we just headed straight for Dunblane, with Strathclyde Police outriders. We were getting more information as we went up the road, about what had happened and about the casualties. The figures were increasing all the time. Then we heard that the perpetrator was also dead, and it was a strange sensation as we drove up towards Dunblane on a route that he must have travelled.'

The two MPs stopped off *en route* to Dunblane to be given a full briefing by police and the Procurator-fiscal at Central Scotland Police HQ in Stirling. The Chief Constable told them they believed the fatalities had now risen to 16.

George Robertson tried to prepare himself for the scenes of grief and heartache which he expected to see at Dunblane Primary – a school where his children had been taught.

'I had been in the school hundreds of times; my three children have all gone through the school. It's not a terribly imposing building; it's fairly plain and ordinary. But we drove up and the place was surrounded by people in various stages of shock. We thought some of them must have been the bereaved parents, but in fact by that stage all those who were affected, or thought to be affected, had been taken to another place. The school was just buzzing with teachers in deep shock. There were a lot of ministers, and other parents around. It was just an amazing atmosphere. I looked at the sign that said "Welcome to our School". I went there for parents' nights and school fêtes, the sort of things that you go to an ordinary school for. It's also a polling station. At every election we would go along and vote in the assembly hall. Because I knew the school there was a complete sense of shock.

'Michael Forsyth's wife had joined us so the three of us were together and we spoke to people. We spoke to Ron Taylor, the head teacher. He came out and gave a graphic description of what had happened and what he'd seen.'

Then the tough-talking politician was asked the question no one could possibly have prepared for: 'Do you want to go into the gym?'

'The Chief Constable asked whether we wanted to go through and see the gymnasium where it had happened. He told Michael Forsyth and me that his men had been in there, but stressed to us that it wasn't going to be easy.

'The school teachers and staff had been in right at the very beginning. The emergency services, including the local health centre doctors, were inside, and staff, who were not used to these sort of major emergencies, had all been there.

'He thought that as we were the policy-makers of the land, we should also see it. We agreed and we were taken to the door of the gymnasium. It is a picture that remains etched in my mind for ever.

'It was a moment of high, immeasurable emotion. You just take it all in but it is very difficult.'

The scene in that gym was a horrific image which will live with the MP for the rest of his life. But he couldn't go off and mourn for the little innocents. He couldn't even go off and shed a private tear over the pointless waste of so many young lives. He had to face the Press.

'We were cautioned about what we could actually say, such as naming the suspected perpetrator, at that point, because the laws in Scotland about evidence are very, very tight. It was a fact that at that stage the outside world did not know all that much. And it transpired that the affected parents, at that stage, didn't know.

'So we went to the Press centre, which was just a vast array of cameras. They were coming in from all around the world. It was very difficult to speak, to know what to say, to try and sum it up. But I think both Michael Forsyth and I felt that we had an obligation to maintain a level of dignity and self-control, as well as a closeness, because that was important, not just because of the events, but because of the way in which the events were going to then be handled.

'There would have been no question about making political points anyway. I think any histrionics or any attempt to grab the stage would simply have been the wrong thing to do. And we both were aware of that, I don't know whether consciously or unconsciously. I don't think we ever said it to each other. We agreed that we weren't going to do anything in the way of interviews unless we did them together, and I think that was one of the factors that had a lot to do with the way the Press itself covered it.

'I was being phoned and pestered right through that Wednesday night by people who wanted to get a political angle on the story.

'But apart from one or two things that had to be done individually, we did everything together. We both refused to do things unless we were doing them together. And where we didn't do things together, it was with the other person's agreement.

'*Newsnight* wanted us to do something live late on in the night and we refused together to do that on the grounds that standing outside in the howling wind is not only undignified but also plays into the hands of instant television. We did have an interview with presenter Kirsty Wark at the Dunblane Hydro hotel.

'From what people told me afterward, I think that one interview had a huge effect on people. Here were two politicians speaking about our feelings, our sentiments, our pain. It was a big signal to the local community and to the wider world. We perhaps showed that politics can be about more than just party advantage.'

It was only when the MP returned to his own family home after a day of high tension, pressure and drama that the full consequences of what had happened began to sink in.

'When I came back to the house I collapsed. I remember that the house was filled with people. The whole family was stunned as well – they knew so many of the people. Everyone was sitting around stunned.

'I really didn't release the emotions until later on the Wednesday night when I was with the family.

'I've not really ever been a highly emotional person. I can't remember crying before. But the events of the day were such that I was in tears at the thought of it. It just suddenly came home with a vengeance.

'I suppose I'd been partly playing a role. You play the part of a public representative. People expect you to give a lead, to be controlled, to react properly in the circumstances. You know that there are going to be huge emotions, but that you are a leader in Scotland.

'The political leaders of Scotland have a job to do and you must to some extent suppress a lot of your own desire to act as normal, private individual. As that day went on, it got more and more difficult to do that. The turmoil inside, especially when we were in the school, and especially when we were shown the gymnasium, was huge and overwhelming.

'As long as you kept yourself going it sort of pushed aside the emotion.'

Somehow George Robertson had to push his pain over the murders to one side and compose himself for the biggest speech of his life – his reply to the Statement to the House of Commons about the tragedy on his own doorstep.

'In the morning I had to start thinking. I was going down to the Commons and I had to speak, make a statement. And of course because life is life, phones went all the time. Parents, family, friends, the Press. They were all phoning. I'd to speak to our party leader Tony Blair and to so many others who wanted to know what was happening, and what was going to happen. It was complete bedlam. But it did help by fending off an awful lot of the sentiment because I was involved and I was doing something. The phones had even gone right through the night. One Australian television company telephoned four times during the night. They were desperate to get me to go on and do something at 5.30 a.m. They were even offering bribes. They said: "We'll give £500, even £1,000 to the school fund, if you'll do it." I was just getting more and more angry with this.

'I remember when I wrote what I was going to say on the plane going down to London. The usual tough, cynical, business executives were reading their newspapers with tears running down their faces.

'But you search for words in the most difficult circumstances. I wrote my speech on the way down, and I tested it on myself.

'The Commons speech the day after the tragedy is probably the toughest speech that I'll ever have to make in my life, and it showed.

'But the moment I arrived in London, I had to go into Tony Blair's office because everyone there wanted to know what was going on. I had my speech typed up there and I remember Alistair Campbell, Tony Blair's press spokesman, being there. There's no tougher, no sharper a newspaper guy than him. I gave the speech to him to read and he said: "That's an excellent speech, George, but you are going to find it very hard to read that. It may have been hard enough to write, but the hardest bit of all is you are going to have to read it."

'And it was very true.

'I then got a call from Michael Forsyth's office to say that he would appreciate it if I went up to join them for the planning meeting they had for the Commons statement on the tragedy. They wanted me to read his statement and to agree it. So I went up. All the Ministers and the Lord Advocate were going over what Michael Forsyth was going to say. I chipped in to their discussion. It's difficult for people to comprehend just how unprecedented that is, but it would just never, never happen in normal circumstances. It has probably never happened before. Then I gave them my speech, and I told them what I was going to say. Michael Forsyth's speech had to be more descriptive and more formal, while mine was essentially quite personal.'

Following Michael Forsyth, George delivered the most difficult speech of his life . . . with the whole world watching.

Wearing a black tie, his voice choked with emotion, he told MPs the impact of the tragedy could not be underestimated.

He said: 'Dunblane today is worse than yesterday in its mourning, and tomorrow will probably be worse still, as the enormity of the massacre comes home in the shape of real children gone, real families afflicted and a whole community scarred and tortured.

'You don't need to have lived in Dunblane or to have seen three children go through Dunblane Primary School to share the grief and the horror and the sheer desolation our town feels today.

'You just have to be a fellow human being.'

Immediately after his statement, he and Michael Forsyth went to see the Prime Minister, to suggest that it would be a good idea if Tony Blair and he came up to Dunblane together the following day.

'I think both the Prime Minister and Tony Blair felt that a joint visit might look like a bit of a political circus rather than a sort of solemn commemoration. But Michael Forsyth and I were absolutely of one mind that they had to come together. It was symbolically important. And, secondly, to do two visits, would have been double the agony and the strain for the people involved. The Prime Minister eventually agreed with that point of view. The two of us then went along to Tony Blair's office and we made the same pitch there.'

So it was agreed that everyone would go to Dunblane together.

Tony Blair and his team planned to stay at the Hilton Hotel in Glasgow, but George declared: 'I'm going home to Dunblane. Do you want to come and stay with me?' He agreed.

'There was a bit of nervousness among the Conservative politicians that Tony Blair was going to be in Dunblane before the Prime Minister. But I told them that Tony was going to be at my home and we were going to be there until we met the Prime Minister the following morning. We gave an absolute assurance that there would be nothing done politically that night. We promised we wouldn't leave the house at night.

'So we went out in the big convoy from Westminster all together. And we were all on the plane together. We parted company at the airport and the Scottish Office car brought us back out to Dunblane. When we arrived at the house we were greeted by my wife. My son and his partner and my other son and daughter were there with some others still watching the news on television and talking. Tony Blair was in our house and normally you would expect that to be a big event, that they had the leader of the Labour Party in the same room, but they just didn't really notice him. They were all so tied up with what was going on in Dunblane that it didn't matter. It was a case of: "Oh yes, someone else is here sort of thing." It wasn't disrespect. It was a sort of Dunblane feeling. People were just hopelessly tied up with the emotions going on at the time. And Tony was so, so deeply affected by it.

'The next day, the day of the Prime Minister and Tony Blair's visit, was easier in a way for Michael Forsyth and me, because we were sort of re-running what had happened and there was someone else to take the focus.

'But it was still emotional, because numbers had become names, names had become people, people had become families. You were beginning to realise the enormity of what had happened. It was the sheer scale. When you multiply one child by their brothers, their sisters, by their parents, by their grandparents, their friends, the circle, the ripple effects that were going out were enormous.

'I said in the House of Commons that people will be asking how it is, and I said: "It is worse today than it was yesterday and it will be worse tomorrow than it was today." That was the case. It just escalated as people began to realise what had happened and the enormity of it all.'

George attended one funeral – he knew the mother of victim Mhairi McBeath.

'Michael Forsyth and I took a decision not to attend all the funerals, because we believed it wouldn't have been fair on the families. The parents wanted the funerals to be private occasions. But Isobel McBeath was a friend whom I'd known before.

'So that was the only one that I went to.

'And I made it clear to others why I only went to that one funeral. And again, I didn't do anything essentially without Michael Forsyth being there. It was still very important that we had the same message as two politicians, and we stuck rigidly to it. I think it was effective and the right thing to do. We were doing what our instincts told us. It was what people wanted us to do and be during this time of tragedy.'

George has a passionate belief that one year on from the massacre the people of Dunblane have begun to heal the scar and are already looking to the future.

'This tragedy is never going to go away and unfortunately it's never going to be allowed to go away. Some of the sentiments shouldn't go away, because you can't forget.

'The lasting memorial has got to be the lessons that are taken from this tragedy, because we must make as sure as we humanly can that this will never happen again.

'The community itself has got a lot of strength. People at the time were talking about the City of Dunblane, which technically it is because it has got a cathedral. But it is highly inappropriate because essentially it is a small town. When you consider the number of fatalities in that community and therefore the effects that that can have, it is quite staggering.

'The person who committed this terrible deed should never be allowed to be the thing that is remembered from the tragedy, because that is what he set out to do, and we have got to make sure that does not happen.

'We have got to make sure that the community ends up stronger and not weaker as a consequence of what has happened. Dunblane Primary School is a good school with a good tradition and a good record. It deserves to be able to come out of this with strength. The heroism that was shown not just by the head teacher, but by other staff at the time, is just beyond belief. They were on the spot at the time and they acted professionally.

'Personally the whole tragedy has had a big impact. I still can't forget so many things . . . the faces of parents, the children. I think in many ways a lot of the other children in Dunblane were deeply affected. The bereaved families, the children who were in the other Primary One class, the children who were absent from school that day for whatever reason, the children who survived and the kids who were injured. They have all been deeply scarred.

'I don't think any of us, Michael Forsyth, the other politicians or I will ever be the same again. I don't think you can go through that without having been shaken to your roots – and yet having your own faith in humanity restored.

'Because this was one act of evil, responded to by a huge act of compassion, courage and bravery. The people who work in the health service dealt with unimaginable circumstances. Unprogrammable circumstances. Unpredictable circumstances. They immediately locked together, responding instantaneously. Even staff who were affected personally just rose to the occasion. The staff at Stirling Royal Infirmary and Falkirk Royal Infirmary. The ambulance crews. The local doctors just around the corner who were on the scene within minutes. But nobody flipped, nobody broke down, nobody among the policemen, and many of them were young and local, nobody among the brave emergency teams. Nobody let the side down despite the pressure that there must have been on them personally.

'What an inspiration that can be. They just put aside their own sentiments and acted as professionals.

'And that I think is something pretty considerable.'

8. A TV PRESENTER

LORRAINE Kelly got into her car to head home. She'd completed another morning slot on breakfast television. The traffic in central London was congested as usual. The car snaked its way through the madness. Her head was buzzing with what had been discussed at the production team's daily meeting. The Paris fashion shows had been talked about. How would GMTV handle the coverage of the annual showcases for the best-dressed? Would they send Lorraine for a live link-up? Would it be pre-recorded?

Before leaving central London that day Lorraine had a photo assignment. A magazine needed a photograph for an interview they'd scheduled for their next issue. Just before noon Lorraine was back in the car heading for home in Berkshire – and toddler daughter Rosie, then aged two.

The radio news was on in the background. Lorraine wasn't paying that much attention to the reports, but she picked up a few key words. School . . . Scotland . . . Shooting . . .

'Was I hearing it right? I called back to the office and asked them if they'd heard anything. I told them I reckoned I'd misheard the report. It was probably in America or somewhere else. I probably wanted to believe I had heard it wrongly. My colleague told me exactly what it was. The whole horrific scenario was confirmed. School, shooting and Scotland. Dunblane. My stomach felt like ice. I couldn't take in what I was hearing. I was born and bred in Scotland, so I suppose major incidents have so much more impact when you know the area. This all seemed too unreal, so unlikely.'

Stunned and finding it difficult to speak, Lorraine listened as her colleague outlined the proposal for the next morning's show. Lorraine and co-presenter Eamonn Holmes would be in Dunblane. The whole programme would be live from the tragic town. Tickets were booked. Hotels organised. Satellite link-ups for a live broadcast already planned. The production team was already on its way to Scotland.

Lorraine and her husband Steve had thought about settling in Dunblane at one point. They were serious enough. It was at a time when Lorraine was between contracts and was unsure where she wanted to be located for work. With Lorraine's family based in and around Glasgow and Steve's in Dundee it was the ideal halfway spot. And Lorraine's passion for Dundee United Football Club meant Dunblane was a well-known point for a comfort stop. She'd always thought of Dunblane with fond memories.

Reflecting on that period when they would quietly wander through the streets, Lorraine said: 'It always had an air of normality and seemed a lovely place to bring up children in safety.'

Over the next hour or so Lorraine packed her case, spent some time with Rosie and then headed for the airport to fly north.

Scotland had been Lorraine's news patch when she first went into the world of TV. She'd worked for TVam – GMTV's forerunner. She was their Scottish reporter and had covered many major stories. After GMTV was launched, Lorraine landed one of the main presenters' jobs on the morning programme. At the time of the tragedy she had her own slot in the late part of the show. The TV exposure made Lorraine a household name and a well-recognised face.

She admits that on first arriving in the town she was apprehensive about the next morning's show.

She said: 'We arrived late afternoon. Once we got ourselves sorted out, we headed to a press conference in the evening. I think that is when it really hit me properly. A policeman started reading out the names of the victims. I thought, when is he going to stop talking? When will he stop reading the names? He just went on and on and on. All these poor children's names. The officer found it really hard to speak. I remember thinking how quiet all the journalists were. Silence, utter silence, everybody was white-faced. Even the hardened old cynics couldn't even speak and everybody went away really quietly. Normally when covering major events the media people will get into little huddles and talk about what's happening. It wasn't like that at all.

'We went back to our hotel and obviously I didn't get any sleep that night because I was thinking about what we were going to do the next day. I was so concerned. I have never been more concerned with a show in my life. It was so important that we got it right. Not for us, not so that we would look good or anything stupid like that, but we really owed it to the local community to get this absolutely right. We had set up a couple of rooms in the hotel as a base. Eamonn and I talked about how we'd do the show. We bounced ideas off each other and tried to work out the best way to handle it. In the end we threw away the scripts and we just busked it.

'There were interviews set up and our colleague Martin Frizell was going to be giving us the latest reports on the aftermath. We had a big team up with us. When the programme started Eamonn turned and asked me about Dunblane. I described what the place is like and pointed out to viewers that this was the last place in the world where you expect something like this to happen. A tragedy such as this happened in other places on the other side of the world. Never in Dunblane. It was so hard. Live TV goes by in a flash and you need to keep your concentration at all times. There was only one point when I nearly lost it. The only time I've ever nearly lost it. We were just heading into a commercial break and I felt I was going to start crying. If the cameras had stayed on me for a second longer, I'd have been crying into every viewer's home. I went off and had a cup of tea. I thought, people don't need this, they don't need to see me crying on air, that's not what I'm supposed to do.'

The rest of the Thursday was spent working on recording reaction from people in the town. She said: 'We filmed some of it in the town; then there was a suggestion that I stood outside the school and record a segment. I couldn't bear that. We decided against the school. Many of the local people came up to us and made it quite clear they did want to speak about this horror on their doorstep.'

In the afternoon Lorraine wrote her weekly column for the *Sunday Post* newspaper. She admits it was hard to write about the horrific events and their aftermath. She didn't sleep well that night.

'On the Friday we did the show in the morning and then I thought, right that's it, now we have to get out and leave these people. I felt we had done our bit and I wasn't keen to hang around and impose ourselves on the community for much longer. The office agreed. I went home on the Friday absolutely distraught. All I wanted to do was get home and give Rosie a cuddle. I just couldn't see past that. I've got to get home to my baby girl. I knew she was fine, but I needed to reassure myself that she was okay.'

When she walked in the door at home, Lorraine's husband Steve told her the police in Dunblane needed to speak with her. She said: 'I couldn't understand why. Had something else happened?'

Constable Ian Hamilton, a police officer assigned to a bereaved family, had contacted GMTV and had been passed on to Lorraine's home. One of the families had watched Lorraine and felt that the way she'd presented her reports and handled the whole tragedy was right. They'd been comfortable with her approach. They wanted to speak to her directly. The grieving mum had made a special request.

Pam and Kenny Ross were in a state of shock. Their five-year-old daughter Joanna had been murdered along with her classmates. Lorraine was asked to call them.

She said: 'I felt so humbled that they wanted to speak to me. I worried about how we'd put out the show, suddenly realising that families of the victims had actually been watching. I immediately offered to do anything I could to help them. I had no idea what I could do apart from talk to them if that is what they wanted. I told the police officer liaising with them I'd drop everything and return to Dunblane immediately. We agreed I'd travel north on the Saturday. It was on the strict understanding that this was a private visit. It had nothing to do with the programme and I wasn't even thinking along these lines.

'Ian Hamilton picked me up at the airport. It was only when we drove to Pam's house that it dawned on me. What would I say? What would I do when I arrived? I wasn't a trained counsellor. What if I said the wrong thing? What if I ended up upsetting them even more – if that was possible?

'I tried to think how I might feel if it had been my daughter. But I couldn't make that leap because it was so sore. Even now I can't imagine because it's too painful. Ian suggested that I just talked. He'd had to listen to me on the journey from the airport so by then he realised I could talk!

'In the panic to get organised I bought a silver frame for Pam, so she could put in a picture of Joanna. I knew she had another little girl, so

I brought along one of Rosie's teddy bears and lots of pictures of Rosie. I didn't even know if that was the right thing to do.

'We arrived at the house in the late afternoon. I walked in and I saw Pam. I don't know what it was, but there was an immediate reaction. We just knew we liked each other and I gave her a huge cuddle and she gave me a cuddle. I just cried my eyes out for ages. Then we sat and we talked and talked and I felt as if I had known her for years. From the early stages we just hit it off together and seemed to have a close affinity. We chatted about our families, our backgrounds and of course about the children. I showed her loads of pictures of Rosie and I gave her the wee things, and she showed me pictures of Joanna. Loads of people were coming in and out of the house that night. It was a strange atmosphere in the house – very calm, very calm. I felt she and Kenny were being so strong. We just kept on talking into the night. We had about 95 cups of tea. Then Pam asked me if I wanted to see Joanna who'd been brought home from the hospital for the few days before her funeral. I felt so honoured to be allowed to see her.

'So I went upstairs and there was this angel lying there in her little Pocahontas nightie, looking perfect. I have never seen a more beautiful child. I howled my eyes out. Pam and Kenny said they would leave me for ten minutes by myself. Her little bedroom was perfect. A real little girlie's bedroom with all her toys and drawings and things around the place. I looked at her and thought I can't believe there is such evil in the world that would do this to all the children and that lovely teacher.

'I came back downstairs and we had more chat and I went away in the wee small hours back to my mum's house. I left my numbers with Pam and told her she could phone me at any time if she wanted. I was staying with my mum in East Kilbride and when I got home I was very upset. My mum is really good and we ended up talking and talking for a long time. Then suddenly, quite late on, the phone rang. It was Pam. I felt glad that she was able to call me. She asked me if I could go to the funeral on the following Monday. The next day, the Sunday, I called the office and told my boss I wouldn't be coming in. I started to tell him why. I was crying and he assured me there was no problem about what I wanted to do. He said I didn't need to explain anything more.

'Joanna and her friend Emma Crozier had a joint funeral. It was a beautiful service. The parents were so strong. So dignified. Pam was worried about me and everyone else.'

The girls' little white coffins lay side by side in Lecropt Church in nearby Bridge of Allan. The girls had been baptised together and since then had been inseparable. The congregation sang 'Jesus Loves Me' – the first hymn the children had learned at Sunday school. The minister, the Reverend William Gilmour, said: 'These two friends were cut down in the evil terror which struck the primary school last Wednesday. It will haunt their parents and us in this community well into the future.'

He recalled how the girls had been christened together on 5 August 1990 in the church. He said: 'That joint baptism may have been a pointer to the fact that thereafter they were to become close friends. To their respective parents each child was precious, loved dearly and cared for tenderly at home. We can appreciate their high hopes for the future womanhood of Emma and Joanna. However, as we are too tragically aware, neither Emma nor Joanna was allowed to fulfil her parents' aspirations.'

Joanna's uncle Gareth spoke of the friendship and fun of both girls. He told mourners how Joanna's grandfather had dressed up as Santa Claus and visited the Sunday school the previous Christmas. When he returned home, Joanna asked if he had been Santa Claus. When he denied it, Joanna pointed out that he was wearing the same shoes as Santa.

Lorraine speaks with a great deal of pride when she refers to her friendship with Pam and Kenny and their families.

'Since then we've kept in touch. We phone regularly and I've been to see them and stayed with the family. The three of them came down and stayed at our place last autumn. Pam is a friend for life and there's no way our friendship will ever stop. We're both such gasbags we would be on the phone for an hour. I always go to the cemetery when I'm in Dunblane. I usually take along some freesias. When Pam was down in London she came to the TV studios for a look around and then we went shopping around London. We had a good time and laughed and talked about Joanna all the time. At the end of the day I could sense that Pam was almost feeling guilty about having enjoyed her day. I told her she shouldn't feel that way at all. Joanna would have wanted her to have a good time.'

The bereaved families organised a memorial service for all 17 victims at Dunblane Cathedral in October – some seven months after the murders. They were careful to ensure everything was how they wanted it. Weeks of meticulous planning went into the event. Prince Charles represented the Queen and the nation, and the families lit candles in memory of each of the children and for Mrs Mayor.

Lorraine had met many more of the families at one of their regular group meetings in the town. During a phone call from Pam, Lorraine was told the group had wanted her to read a special poem and then each of the victims' names as the candles were lit. The families wanted her to play a part in the memorial service which was to be televised live by the BBC.

'This was such a special honour – to be asked to play a part in their memorial service.'

On the eve of the service Lorraine and the others taking part had a rehearsal.

'I knew I had to get it right for the children and for Gwen. I'm not used to reading out loud in large buildings, so I had difficulty with that initially. But suddenly the words just wouldn't come out. I was so choked up. I physically couldn't speak. I managed to blunder my way through the reading. But then it came to the names at the rehearsal and I couldn't do it. I was so worried I'd let people down. We ran through all the practical stuff about who was where and at which moment during the service. But the next morning my nerves were in tatters. I asked Pam if I could go to Joanna's room and read my piece out loud. I knew I had to do that to get over whatever hurdle I was facing. I sat there on her bed, imagining her wee face and all the rest of them. I said: "Right, this is what we're going to have to do and it's for you." I read it out and got through it without breaking down. I honestly believe had I not done that I would never have managed it in the cathedral.

'To read each victim's name as their family lit a candle was so emotional. I stood there with my fingernails digging into the palm of my hand urging myself to keep control. It was difficult for me, but God only knows how difficult it must have been for each and every member of the families.'

More than 600 people attended the service. They filed into the cathedral in the hour or so before the service was due to commence.

Inside, the congregation heard the Very Reverend Professor James Whyte say: 'Even in the darkest night we must look for and long for the light.'

Before each family lit their candle, he added: 'The candle is a good symbol, especially for the children. It is small yet it is a bright, warm light.' He added that the candle is also a symbol of fragility and vulnerability.

'It is easily snuffed out. Such is our life and the life of a child. When someone dies young, we tend to think of what might have been. Children change so quickly, but these will change no more. Yet we value them for what they were, not for what they might have been. They gave us light for a little time, and we remember that light with thankfulness. Apart from that I have a strange feeling that age doesn't matter very much in Heaven. Those who lost a dear one, those whose lives are scarred, have their journey to make. And all of us who share the horror must make our journey into a safer, more civilised society. When things like this happen, you find yourself cast in a new role – bereaved parents, bereaved family. It is unbearably painful, but it also confers a certain distinction, importance, a new identity.

'You are a victim and it is a dreadful experience, but you cannot let what happened become your whole identity. We must never give our other children the impression that, to be valued, a child must be dead. That is to close your door against life. I don't think we will ever have a satisfying explanation of why such terrible things happen, why they happen to us, why they happen to innocent children. But no loss is a dead loss – in all loss there is gain. Each candle represents a unique human life. They were different from one another, those bright little buttons. So are we all different from one another and no one can dictate the route we must follow in our journey from darkness to light. I cannot tell you how the light will return. But as long as we stand still, none of us will find it.'

And the Reverend Colin McIntosh told the memorial service: 'I hope the whole nation, perhaps even the world, will remember Dunblane in the end not for the tragedy that has taken place here – but for the way its people met and overcame it.'

The poem for Lorraine's reading was called 'Little Child Lost'. Lorraine made a few alterations to the original piece by Eugene G. Merryman Jr.

Here is the version she read out at Dunblane Cathedral.

> *Shall we ever find anything other than a child that can be such a paradox in our lives? A little person that can generate such a conflict of anger and love.*
>
> *One that causes so much sorrow when they have been hurt, only to cause so much happiness with their laughter.*
>
> *One who can cause so much fear for their safety and well-being, and then so much comfort and serenity when they are asleep in your arms.*
>
> *This little person has the ability to pull at each and every emotion known to us and some that we weren't even aware we had.*
>
> *When the loss of a child happens, no matter how, what do we do then? Will we ever escape the sound of their voice? Will we never stop catching a glimpse of them out of the corner of our eye?*
>
> *The answer is that you do see and you do hear, just as you continue to love, for that child was part of your soul.*
>
> *Although you may not always hear them, as they move upon the wings of the wind, nor may you always see them as they go past on a ray of sunlight, be assured they are with you.*
>
> *Though we may never be able to explain your loss or console you, I wish to thank you, for without your child, and other children who have gone before us, there would be no children in Heaven.*
>
> *Playing where they never tire, your child is safe and happy.*

'When I sat down Mick North, whose daughter Sophie died, gave me a hug and I couldn't even give him a hug back because I thought, if I give him a hug back, I'll just start howling. I sat there on the pew all hunched up literally trying to keep myself together. Afterwards Pam gave me a big hug and said: "I'm so proud of you. Thank you very much."

'At Christmas I was opening my presents and there was a little box. A card attached said: "To Lorraine, thank you so much. This is from all the families."

'Inside, there was a silver pin shaped like a snowdrop. It was specially made. I was so touched. I still find it difficult to accept that there is anything for them to be grateful to me about. It has been a privilege to meet the families. I think they conducted themselves so well and with such dignity and grace when actually they had been kicked in the teeth so much.'

Lorraine recalls a visit to Pam's house when she was with her in Joanna's room.

'Pam had just got Joanna's clothes back and all her bits and pieces from that day. There was her play-piece, a packet of crisps and things like that. Pam asked me to look at the window and there were little fingerprints on the glass. Can anyone really imagine not being able to clean a window because they didn't want to remove their child's fingerprints?

'I just don't know how they deal with it, I really don't. I'm sure they all have terrible days. It is an experience which affected me an awful lot. I still get flashbacks of Dunblane and of that first day when we were there and realised what exactly had happened in the school.

'One of my favourite sayings is that life is too short. If Pam's taught me anything – as well as being my pal – it is to be more easy-going. If things aren't going well I just always try to see what is good in something. It puts a lot of things into perspective.

'On the Monday night after Joanna's funeral, I was an absolute wreck. Who wouldn't be? But I got home and I just sat with Steve and talked and talked until I got it all out of my system. The next day I had to go back into work and it was my normal programme. It's live, it's lovely, it's fluffy, it's fashion, it's sort of jolly and all that.

'I suddenly thought, I can't do this. I remember sitting in make-up and wondering how, after having been to the funeral, I could sit there and not say anything at all about the previous day.

'In the end I just said that I wanted everybody to know, particularly everybody in Dunblane, and particularly Pam and Kenny, that we are all thinking of you. I added that because I was then going to do something completely different and unconnected to the tragedy, it didn't mean that we were not thinking of them. I just about managed to hold that together, took a deep breath, did a link into a bit of tape. That gave me time to take a big deep breath. I couldn't go on after that wee girl's funeral and say nothing. I realised

I had my job to do but it was so important for me to mention Dunblane.

'I know Dunblane and the aftermath will be part of my life for ever.'

A picture of Joanna sits in Lorraine's dressing-room at the GMTV studios. She treasures the friendship she has forged with the little girl's parents. But she said: 'I wish I had known them in different circumstances. I wish I'd known Joanna. In a way, because of what had to happen before we became friends, I wish we weren't and Joanna was still here.'

9. A JOURNALIST

'DO you want to go to Dunblane?' The question came from *Sunday Mail* editor Jim Cassidy seconds after he'd been given early reports of the devastation at the primary school. On the receiving end was women's editor and columnist Melanie Reid.

Melanie had been sitting among a group of newspaper executives at a Wednesday morning planning conference. It was a routine weekly event designed to throw up ideas for stories, features and photographs for the following Sunday's paper.

'My colleague Peter Samson, the paper's chief reporter – and a co-author of this book – interrupted the conference,' she recalled.

'It's a rare event for anyone to interrupt. He just said quietly: "A gunman has gone into a school in Dunblane and killed some children. They're saying as many as eight are dead. It's chaotic."

'We were all stunned. As journalists we're all used to things happening quickly, to responding to sudden, dramatic, sometimes harrowing events.

'We read on the wires regularly about stuff like that happening in California. But nothing prepares you for something like that in your own back garden.

'Nothing prepares you for the jolt from the mundanity of a Wednesday conference . . . to the simply indescribable – happening just up the road. It does involve a kind of warp, a transition from the before to the after, when nothing can be the same again.'

A reporter and photographer had already been dispatched to Dunblane as soon as the news desk heard what was happening. They had left the newspaper's Glasgow headquarters and were on the 40-minute journey to Dunblane. The editor decided to send more staff.

'I remember how he asked me, almost hesitantly, if I wanted to go too. Normally editors don't ask: they tell. But Jim's face was twisted with shock and compassion and, in a funny way, I felt some of it was for the person he was asking to do the job.'

Melanie left the office with photographer Ronnie Anderson. Less than two hours had passed since the first shot had been fired.

'In a daze, we set off up the road. I have an acute memory of sitting hunched in the front seat of Ronnie's car, listening intently to Radio 5, keen to pick up any snippet of information to build up a bigger picture of what had actually happened.

'Ronnie's is one of those cars where the cigarette ash and the nicotine stains and the unopened phone bills come halfway up the windows. Normally we joke about these things; but that day we sat in silence, concentrating fiercely on the radio.

'As we left Glasgow, we heard that crash teams of doctors were being rushed by police from the city's Yorkhill hospital. The hospital treats children and is well known for its medical expertise. They would be on the same road as us. Indeed they were. Within seconds they swept past us, sirens blaring. They had the fast lane all to themselves.

'On the outskirts of Dunblane, we were held up by roadworks. As we sat at the temporary traffic lights, the radio announcer broke the news that it was a Primary One class.

'I remember both Ronnie and I gasped involuntarily. It somehow made it so much worse. "Look behind," said Ronnie; in the stationary car behind, the woman passenger, presumably listening to the same report, had covered her distraught mouth in her hands, as if to stifle her anguish.'

The two journalists drove into Dunblane and parked.

'Did we know what to expect? Did we have any concept of the awfulness, the darkness, the savage sight of naked grief? Of course not. We were as unprepared in a psychological sense as we were physically unprepared for the bone-chilling cold. It was one of those days when the cold strikes up through the soles of your shoes as if they're cardboard.

'We left the car in the crowded supermarket car park. It was not yet lunch-time. The news had not yet reached everyone, and so there they were, buying their bread and their cornflakes and their mince.

'It was an image of ordinariness, of comfort, of normality,

juxtaposed with horror, that was to occur again and again.

'In the road outside the school, parents were still milling, waiting for news of their children. Those who had been safely reunited were leaving the school by the bottom gate. I remember acutely the poignant image of small women carrying children far too big to be carried.

'Everyone was crying. We saw one middle-aged woman come out and run towards friends, her face crumpled with joy: "They're safe," she shouted. They stood hugging. For a brief moment photographers jostled and snarled at each other as they tried to capture the image. That unruly, insatiable beast, the media, was beginning to flex its muscles. But there was no feeding frenzy. The usual matiness and sense of reunion that graces big media gatherings, when reporters and photographers greet friends they haven't seen since the last disaster, was totally absent. Cynicism was at least temporarily in abeyance. We greeted each other with nods, and silence. There was an eerie sense of respectfulness, of a Press pack for the first time subdued by the nature of what it faced. We had lost our appetite.

'One raw young freelance came bouncing out of the crowd. "Hallo Melanie!" she said brightly, with a smile on her face, excited at being at the big event. I was embarrassed by her insensitivity.

'As we stood, behind hastily-erected barriers at the gates of the school, I felt a sense of inadequacy, of indecency. We saw the despair on the faces of queuing parents. We could almost reach out and touch the police cars that rushed out bearing the bereaved. We were too close. I saw photographers, tough, hard, selfish professionals, with tears in their eyes. I saw a local policeman I knew. He had been crying. His face was marked with horror and bewilderment.

'Did any of us know what to write? I think not. What could we say? We all faced the same problem, trying to find words for something that simply defied description. I envied the news-gatherers from daily papers, the people preoccupied with the who, when and how of day-to-day journalism. For those of us feature writers, who had to lift the dark skirts of the tragedy and try to climb underneath, it was hard.

'Like almost every mother in the country, I felt an overwhelming, irrational desire to phone my own young son Douglas, in Primary Two in a country school miles away. I wanted to leave, to stop watching such unbearable grief.

'As a distraction I remember concentrating on the names of the houses up the road to the school, big wealthy Victorian villas, with sturdy, pretentious, middle-class names. The illusion of security in stone and mortar was terribly exposed as just that – an illusion.

'Seeking information rather than alcohol, we ended up watching Sky TV in a pub near the station. Sitting there, transfixed by the running story on TV, we encountered trouble. A group of angry, boozy locals came in. They saw Ronnie's camera gear, nestling with intent on a bar seat. They saw my notebook folded in my coat pocket. And as we sat at the bar they stood close behind us, crooning obscenities, calling us scum, vultures, parasites and worse. Daring us to respond. The air clouded with intimidation. But it was understandable. The locals, unable to vent their anger on the perpetrator of the atrocity, had turned it on the nearest convenient target – the Press. There was a feeling of naked hostility, of violence only just kept in check. Gathering as much dignity around us as we could, we fled back out into the cold. The episode had merely added to the surreal atmosphere.

'Dunblane came to symbolise this terrible feeling of disjunction between what should be and what was. It was as if life had shattered and yet everyone was carrying on as normal. Trains still ran into the station. Dogs still got walked. People did things because they thought they ought to. All of us went through the motions. Press conferences were held, but they were empty gestures, for the people at the very heart of the tragedy would never face a Press conference.

'Politicians struggled as much as anybody. I admired both Michael Forsyth, the Secretary of State for Scotland and local MP, and George Robertson, his Shadow and local resident, for, just once, taking off their political overcoats, for setting aside the essential survival kit of the parliamentarian; the bluff and the half-truth, the party-honed responses. Later that week, Prime Minister John Major and Labour leader Tony Blair indulged in the same simple symbolism of travelling together, expressing their grief together. Their message was, party politics is irrelevant, insignificant. For a time at least.

'The watching world needed them to do this. In what became a most extraordinary national spasm of grief, the like of which none of us could remember, people were grateful to politicians and Royals for representing them.

A MOTHER'S SORROW . . . Kareen Turner in the conservatory at her home. She desperately misses her daughter Megan (inset) and says: 'She lives in the hearts of everyone who knew her.'

ALONE WITH HIS MEMORIES . . . Rod Mayor sits by the rockery at his home in Bridge of Allan. His murdered wife Gwen (inset) loved to spend her summer lunch time breaks in the garden.

SADNESS AND SOLITUDE . . . Dr Mick North in his kitchen surrounded by paintings by daughter Sophie (right). She gave him the strength to carry on after the death of his wife, Barbara.

BATTLING ON . . . Pam Ross moved into the public spotlight in the guns campaign after the death of daughter Joanna (inset). She says: 'I did it for Joanna, her classmates and their teacher.'

WORDS OF COMFORT . . . The Reverend Colin McIntosh of Dunblane Cathedral spent hours walking in the streets speaking to locals in the aftermath of the tragedy.

THE FACE OF HOPE . . . Little Coll Austin, critically injured in the Dunblane Primary School gym, battled against the odds to survive. Now the plucky youngster loves nothing better than playing football with his dad in the garden.

LUCKY TO BE ALIVE . . . Gym teacher Eileen Harrild came eye-to-eye with the murderer before he shot her four times. As she lay injured she feared she was close to death.

FOR LITTLE MEGAN . . . Victim Megan Turner's gran Nancy McLaren tends to the flowers at the little one's grave. Nancy wrote a special tribute to Megan which was read out at her funeral in Dunblane Cathedral.

'At another Press conference, it became comic. Council officials were rolled out to feed the Press – you could almost hear the police liaison guy in the backroom saying, get someone for Christ's sake, saying anything, just keep the Press happy. One man was an official with a body which, because of local government reorganisation, was shortly to cease to exist; another was not officially in post for two weeks. Would the gym be pulled down? What about school security? They could not speak for an authority which did not yet exist. These decisions were not theirs to make.

'We listened politely. It would never see the light of day in newsprint; but in the same way that people make tea when there's a death in the house, so journalists, police liaison officers and bureaucrats kept talking. It helped everyone. It gave us all something to do, made us feel less helpless.'

Melanie joined the *Sunday Mail* nearly ten years ago. She was no stranger to reporting disasters. She helped to cover the Lockerbie disaster, when the Pan Am jet crashed on the Borders town. And she was in Aberdeen to cover the Piper Alpha North Sea tragedy.

'Covering disasters doesn't become easier because you've done it before. If anything, you begin to feel even more inadequate because you realise how useless words are. In a professional sense, Dunblane was uniquely self-contained. The mayhem was over, the perpetrator was dead, all in a matter of a morning. Whereas Lockerbie and Piper Alpha were merely the start of years of journalistic investigation, in Dunblane the follow-ups were limited. In the horror of its simplicity, Dunblane was, hopefully, unique.'

By the Saturday afternoon, Melanie had written her copy for that Sunday's paper. Here is what she wrote:

> *Today, with an irony so dreadful it stills our soul, is Mother's Day. Even in Dunblane.*
>
> *And inside Gwen Mayor's deserted Primary One classroom lie the cards that will never be finished.*
>
> *Every mum knows those adorably haphazard offerings from Primary Ones*
>
> *Those smudged infant images, those daubs of bright colour from little hands that aren't yet quite sure which*

hand to hold the paintbrush in, let alone write.

Those little fragments of love that mums never throw out, but cherish and hoard, tucking away in drawers with a secret smile.

But no more.

For the bereaved mothers of Dunblane, waking up not to a cuddle and a sticky kiss but to emptiness, those joys are gone forever.

Four days on, it is still too much for any of us to take in.

For days we have all struggled to cope, trying to reconcile the ordinariness of this sturdy, stone-built Scottish town with the extraordinary horror of what happened last Wednesday.

Those who represent the community – church ministers, civic leaders, councillors, people right up to the level of the Scottish Secretary, the Prime Minister – and today even the Queen – have come and bravely tried to fill the void.

The nation itself, shaken by a spasm of grief unknown in modern times, has cause to be grateful to them for their dignity, for their ability to mouth words of sorrow when the rest of us were incapable of speech.

Police and ambulance crews, desensitised by years of dealing with disaster, have been shaken to their very core.

Journalists have struggled too, in a way I have never seen before.

The kind of reporters and photographers who chew rocks for breakfast have been unable, for once, to find comfort in cynicism.

It is as if humanity's defences have been laid bare, as if all the things which we thought mattered have been taken away from us, as if our foundations have cracked.

Under such circumstances, life itself becomes reduced to a series of fractured images.

On the dreaded morning of the massacre, distraught parents ran up and down Doune Road to the primary school.

I remember seeing a grandmother in a brown coat, her face twisted with tears of joy, arms outstretched. 'We got our boys. They are home,' she shouted, collapsing into the arms of a man.

Doune Road, where there is a Neighbourhood Watch scheme to guard against bad men, where the gracious Victorian villas bear names like Morven, Dreemskerry, Ramornie, where the crocuses herald spring. THE MASSACRE MAKES A MOCKERY OF IT ALL.

I remember seeing a policeman outside the school break with the strain, and bury his head in his hands in private agony.

And I remember the mothers running in bath-robes and slippers, their hands clamped across their mouths to keep the anguish in.

The same mothers coming out later, carrying children far too big to be carried, holding them so tight it hurt.

The father in his mechanic's overalls, called away from servicing a car.

I saw a nun in tears. I saw an old man adjusting a child's gloves in the bone-chilling cold, a gesture of normality amidst the madness.

I saw a photographer put down his lens, blinded by tears, thinking of his own child in Primary One in a school just a few miles away.

The next day I remember the sight of macho building-site workers, in hard hats and boots, unselfconscious to be seen carrying flowers in public.

But this was a week when grown men wept as openly as women, hugged each other freely.

People said odd things, their brains melted with shock. 'What will this mean for the town? For our reputation?' said one woman. 'I mean, I can't buy Lockerbie butter to this day.'

'It would be more acceptable if they had been wiped out in a motorway pile-up,' said a man. And somehow you know what he meant.

Then there was the window of the Dunblane video shop, decorated with a giant X Files sign, an unwelcome reminder that truth is stranger than fiction. That this town will not need horror movies for a long, long time.

As the hours wore on, the people slowly retreated behind their front doors.

Dunblane is not a town that likes drawing attention to itself.

After the initial panic, there was no screaming and wailing, no biblical beating of breasts.

But the anguish crept from the cold stone. And by then the terrible stories were piling up on themselves.

Of Dr Kathryn Morton, working at Stirling Royal Infirmary when her daughter was killed.

Of Isobel McBeath who lost her husband . . . and now had lost her little girl. Of Michael North who lost his wife two years ago . . . and now his little Sophie.

It went on and on.

By the end of the week the media circus, that ever-present accoutrement of modern tragedy, had come to town.

As the locals retired indoors they were replaced on the streets by TV crews and international Press from China, Germany, Denmark.

CBS TV crews from the States arrived in a flurry of chauffeur-driven cars.

I watched the female presenter sit in the back of the limo doing her lipstick, checking her hair, tuning her face to compassion mode.

Dunblane was number one on the world news schedule all right.

There was a Spanish crew anxious to find the gun range where the perpetrator practised his evil obsession.

But that is something Dunblane is not interested in. The townsfolk are not ready to turn their thoughts to the man who raped them.

They don't want to know, don't want to talk about him, to hear about his evil background. They whisper of him, refuse to speak his name.

There is too much hurt to be absorbed, too much loss to come to terms with first.

Like wounded animals they flocked to their beautiful 13th century cathedral, seeking the comfort of a late night vigil.

For Dunblane's bereaved, it will get worse before it gets

better. As the numbness wears off and the shock fades, the pain will get stronger.

Reality, this Mother's Day, means the indescribable ache of empty arms.

And that reverberating, unanswerable, searing question, that shakes the very core of this ancient place:

WHY?

Melanie's copy ran on the centre pages of the *Sunday Mail* that weekend. On the front page a large photograph of victim Megan Turner was used to help launch an anti-guns petition and campaign.

Over a period of about three weeks a staggering 428,279 signatures were collected. The response was unprecedented in newspaper terms. Completed petitions were sent in from all over the world.

After much thought the paper decided to make an approach to a group of the bereaved parents and their families. They were invited to travel to London to present the boxloads of the completed petition to the Home Secretary, Michael Howard, and to Michael Forsyth. In many ways it was an ambitious request. Those approached agreed. Politicians agreed to meet the group at the Houses of Parliament.

Flights were booked. A coach was organised to transfer the party from Heathrow Airport to the city centre. Lunch was laid on at the Waldorf Hotel.

Editor Jim Cassidy was there. The paper was also represented by political editor Angus Macleod, chief reporter Peter Samson and photographer Ronnie Anderson. Melanie, too.

As well as the parents of several victims, two sets of grandparents travelled, along with Esther Mayor, daughter of the murdered schoolteacher. For many it was the first time they had left Dunblane since the tragedy; for some it was their first trip to London; for one the first time flying.

Melanie admitted she was uncomfortable as the day of the trip dawned. She said: 'I had mixed feelings. I'm sure everyone in the group did. I felt embarrassment, the feeling of intrusion on private grief. The wish that I wasn't there.

'I drove to Dunblane and joined the bus there for the journey to Edinburgh Airport. As I got on I remember dipping my head, avoiding anything but the briefest eye contact with the bereaved parents – almost as you do to someone who is badly handicapped. I remember feeling dreadfully nervous.

'I sat in silence. Small talk was impossible. So was big talk. How can you talk about inconsequential things to people who have lost so much? The weather? The journey? How can you insult them by being so banal? But you can't mention their loss, can you? Can't make any reference to their children? The day it happened? Their feelings? It was unthinkable.

'Then a strange thing happened. Here I was, shut in a minibus with people who had walked through death's dark vale, and then they started laughing and joking about not being able to smoke on the bus. It was an extraordinary ice-breaker, and it was great to be able to turn round and meet their eyes and laugh. I began to relax.

'But the irony did not escape me. They were putting me at ease, instead of vice versa. As the day progressed, I went through a fast learning process. I learnt that these suffering people had developed a collective bond, a group strength, the courage to laugh and talk and live again. They were jolly, cheery, funny, making an enormous effort for OUR sakes. They also reduced me to tears with their ability to talk openly and lovingly about their lost children. I remember sitting opposite a mother and father, who'd lost their respective little girls, as we bumped along London's Embankment.

'"I saw her last night, you know," said the father, almost casually. "She showed herself to me."

'"Did she turn round? Have you seen them? Are they growing?" replied the mother. "My little one's wings are quite big now."

'I did a mental double-take. It took me a few seconds to realise it was a shared fantasy about their children in heaven. I held my breath, tears rolling openly down my face, choked at the suffering of these people, the anguish that could produce moments of almost beautiful poignancy. When they saw I was crying they stopped, apologising for upsetting me. Again I had the weird feeling of role reversal.

'Later on in the day, it became almost riotous as Kenny Ross, whose daughter Joanna had died, lifted our mood as we sat at lunch. He was hilarious. Our end of the table was noisy, rather than hushed. Kenny teased me relentlessly after the waiter called me sir, and it provoked much merriment. In amongst it all they talked openly and beautifully about their loss and Esther Mayor talked about her mother Gwen, and about missing all the hugs that had given her strength in the days immediately after the tragedy.'

That morning the group had met Tony Blair. The families sat around a huge meeting table as Mr Blair and senior colleagues addressed them. A camera crew – present with the families' approval – filmed discreetly in the background. Our group wanted to express their opposition to gun ownership. At times the sound of suppressed sobbing filled pauses in the proceedings.

After lunch we travelled to Whitehall and Dover House, the Scottish Office's London HQ. Inside, a small group of civil servants buzzed about.

'One bureaucrat was proving difficult, power-broking, trying to put obstacles in the way. I remember my feeling of contempt for the woman, who showed no concern for the group sitting outside in the coach, waiting patiently.'

Minutes later the Scottish Secretary arrived on the scene from a door next to the grand staircase in the hallway. He whispered in the ear of his civil servant. There was a frenzy of activity. The Prime Minister wanted to see the group. He was in 10 Downing Street. He wanted to discuss the guns issue with the families.

Melanie recalls: 'There was a problem. We'd achieved the near impossible, getting to the PM, and then we lost one of the group. Megan Turner's dad Willie was nowhere to be seen. Panic ensued. His wife Kareen looked flustered as the rest of the party began to wind its way out towards the rear gardens of Dover House to the rear entrance to Number Ten.

'Then Kareen shouted: "He must be on the bus. He's maybe in the loo." My colleague Peter Samson went to investigate and sure enough the toilet door in the bus was shut. Peter called: "Willie! Hurry up – the Prime Minister is waiting for you!" The door opened, Willie's head popped out, looking puzzled. The words hit him. He ran from the bus and dashed into the high-security warren of Downing Street.

'Later he laughed as we told him he'd never have anyone shout that to him in the loo again. It was a lighter moment in a difficult day.

'Coming home on the bus from Edinburgh Airport I remember sitting opposite Mick North, seeing the pain in his face when he shut his eyes, and having to avert my eyes, feeling like a voyeur. Earlier I had been stilled as he spoke about losing both his only child and his wife. "There is no one to tell me not to bite my nails now," he said. "Sophie used to sit beside me in the car and tell me off for it." His grief and anguish were like a physical presence. I wanted to hug him because, for him, there truly were no words. He had nobody.

'On that bus, in the dark, the energy and commitment that had buoyed up the party throughout the day began to evaporate. They fell silent, their faces grew sad. Their memories crowded back. I was reminded of a paralysed girl I had met who told me about the aftermath of her accident. You put on a clown's mask, she said. You keep smiling even when you're crying inside. After a while, you even begin to kid yourself.

'For those parents, the clown's mask had not been in place long enough for any kidology. And as they grew tired, and the dark crept in, it slipped.

'As we drove towards the hills north of Stirling, one of the parents rose from her seat and said she wanted to say a few words. My colleagues all glanced at each other in apprehension. What was coming? Was there a problem? But she wanted to thank us for taking them to London, for arranging that they could meet the country's most powerful people.

'We were stunned. They were thanking US? They were the ones who deserved the thanks for making the effort to leave the security of their homes and take part in the handover. A granny in the party, who had flown for the first time, was quite overwhelmed by the day's events. She couldn't believe all that she had done and packed into one day. She turned and said: "It's been a wonderful day – but for all the wrong reasons."

'Later that week I wrote about their courage and their dignity. But I remember being terrified of sounding patronising. The bereaved in Dunblane have passed through a door that none of the rest of us can ever pass through. What they feel we cannot even begin to imagine. And we must pay them the ultimate compliment and respect that.

'Did the Press learn anything from Dunblane? I think we all learnt, even the most hard-bitten of us, that we still have the capacity for self-restraint. And I hope the outside world, who regard many journalists as a lower form of pond life, learnt that too. The Press in Dunblane showed – and are still showing – amazing restraint.

A JOURNALIST

'Dunblane was a disaster in a media age. The town filled up with hardware – satellite dishes, the bleep of mobile phones and wire machines, the paraphernalia of broadcasting. But nobody, thank God, forgot that the tragedy was about the ultimate software – human beings.'

10. A CHURCHMAN

HIS dark eyes seem to search deep into your soul, seeking out your innermost thoughts. He speaks slowly, almost ponderously, easing out every word and caressing it before it leaves his mouth.

The Reverend Colin McIntosh has been talking a great deal over the last year . . .

But he has also been listening. Listening to the people who need him most – the people of Dunblane . . . His people.

Colin McIntosh is a giant of a man, both in stature and in the way he's respected by people of this tiny cathedral city.

But the last 12 months have weighed heavily on Colin McIntosh's wide shoulders.

As one of Dunblane's dedicated churchmen, and minister at the cathedral itself, he's had to dig deep into his own faith and beliefs to try to support and guide those touched by evil.

A year after the massacre in Dunblane Primary School gym, Colin McIntosh still walks the streets daily.

'Just in case anyone just wants to talk,' he says.

The community of Dunblane has had to reach deep into the well of Christian faith in search of comfort. They held hands in the pews of Dunblane Cathedral on Mothering Sunday, four days after they'd been robbed of their innocents, their future.

They mourned together as the names of the 16 tiny schoolchildren and their teacher echoed around the 13th-century building. They are still holding hands a year on; supporting each other; helping each other; crying with each other; facing the future together.

Colin McIntosh has questioned his own faith many times since that blackest of days. And he has cried with the people of Dunblane. He cried as he comforted the heartbroken parents of little Hannah Scott minutes after they'd been told she was dead. He cried for their grief. He cried because he had baptised little Hannah.

'If there were times when I felt I had lost hold of anything I believed in, at the same time I had the sense that there was something holding me. While I was saying: "God, why? Why?" there was something else, something deeper holding me.'

The morning of 13 March 1996 was unusual. Colin McIntosh wasn't in his parish, not at his manse nestling in the shadow of the cathedral.

As fate would have it, he'd driven out of the town heading for Dundee to pick up a new car, reaching the outskirts of Dunblane around the same time as hell was breaking out in the school gym.

'I left Dunblane just before 10 a.m. not knowing that anything had happened. It must have been sheer chaos round at the school at that time. Then as I was driving out of Dundee sometime after 11 a.m., I thought: "Let's see what the radio is like in this car." I turned it on and immediately heard a news flash about shootings in Dunblane.

'There were no details at that stage about how many had been killed or injured.

'I'll always remember my reaction. I thought: "There must be another Dunblane somewhere."

'As the report went on, I realised they were talking about MY Dunblane. But I thought: "Dunblane is the last place where something like this would happen."

'I thought: "Why was I away when this happened?" I had a tremendous feeling of guilt that I wasn't actually in my parish when this terrible thing was taking place.

'The radio report said it had happened at the primary school so I knew where to head for. I think I'll always remember driving down to Dunblane with mixed feelings of disbelief and guilt. I couldn't believe what had happened.

'I was terrified at what I was about to drive into. I went straight to the school. I couldn't get parked anywhere near, so I just abandoned the car.

'The Doune Road was absolutely mobbed with people, many of them coming in the opposite direction, very distressed. I just ran towards the school as fast as I could.

'The area around the school was cordoned off and there were crowds of people everywhere. I was able to push my way through and as soon as one of the policemen saw my dog-collar he let me in right away. I was shown along to the staffroom, because that's where the parents had been taken to wait for news. There were one or two other local ministers there when I arrived.'

He didn't know it then, but Colin was to spend hours in that room amid harrowing scenes of heartache, tears and tragedy as the families waited for news.

'I knew some of the parents personally and I knew others from seeing them around town. I'd picked up a little information before I'd gone into the room and I knew these were the parents of the children concerned, but I didn't know why they were being kept in the room, so we were all really just guessing. At that stage I didn't know that a teacher had been killed. I didn't know how many children had been killed. I didn't know which ones. I didn't know whether there were any injured. I didn't know if the parents in that room had lost a child. I later found out that they were in that room because they HAD lost a child.

'We really weren't getting any information at all, but I can't criticise the police for that. I saw how distressed they were and I began to pick up some hints that they were having difficulty with identification and that must have added to their stress. The other ministers and I didn't know what we should do. We didn't know what sort of line we should take.

'At first we were trying to reassure parents, telling them: "I'm sure it will be all right," but as time went on and we began working some things out for ourselves, we began to fear the worst. We began to realise that all these parents in there beside us were there because their child had been killed. Then the police started to call out the parents' names. Slowly. One by one. Numbness had taken over us all, and I can recall finding it very difficult to think clearly.

'We tried to attend to all the practical things. There was a mother there who had a young baby who needed changing. There were some children who needed to be amused in some way. You try to deal with those kinds of things, the small, trivial things you could cope with because you couldn't actually take in the full reality of the situation. So I suspect, maybe to my shame, that I really hadn't started at that stage thinking through "what are we going to do now?"

'The parents just wanted to know why they were being kept waiting. "What if it's my child?" was all they could say. Understandably, there was a lot of anger building up, and most of that was being directed against the police. Once or twice a senior officer came in and he tried to reassure, but he just got pretty rough treatment, although I'm sure he was capable of taking that and would understand the reasons. It was just pent-up anger.

'I think it really began to dawn on everyone when the police and social workers started calling families through. The room went quiet because we were waiting for the next group to open the door and call someone out. It was a case of "who's next?", "who would be called?", "what were they going to be told?" It did go oh so quiet at that stage.

'I suppose all the ministers just continued as best we could. To be honest, I really don't know how much help we were. I suspect maybe it was just the knowledge that there were one or two other people there with them that might have helped in some way.

'I felt totally inadequate, but we stayed until the last set of parents had been taken out.'

The minister and the rest of Dunblane's clergymen then gathered in the school's dining-room area.

'I'll always remember there was one group of all the clergymen and there was another group of all the doctors, and we were standing there with nothing to do.

'The police were still racing around, but all the parents were in separate rooms with their counsellors, police and social workers. We were just left, and we stood feeling utterly useless. There was no role for us now. Several things were raised as we stood there, starting to try and think.

'We agreed we had to try and find out the names of those who had died, because we wanted to make contact with the families. The police said they would get us a list as soon as possible. It was just taken for granted that we would work together on this, but we didn't quite know what the next few hours held for us.

'We began to talk about the necessity of us all to have a meeting later on that day to begin to plan together what we were going to do. I think that really was as far as we got, at that stage, as some of the parents began to come out after being told about their children.

'I can remember being confronted with one couple I knew well. Hannah Scott's parents. I had baptised Hannah. I just happened to meet them and that was pretty awful. That really helped to drive it home for me. Here was a wee girl I had actually baptised. All I could do was hug them. We couldn't do anything but cry together.

'I left the school, but it took me quite a while to get home. I was meeting an awful lot of people. They were just stopping and hugging each other in the streets. Tears were flowing and there were tremendous, unforgettable scenes of distress.

'I was simply one of them who was feeling exactly the same as they did. I don't think it was a question of trying to comfort or reassure people, or say: "We must try to be strong." It really was just a question of trying to be there for them, and I certainly wasn't fit for any more than that.'

Colin arrived at the manse to be confronted by a sea of reporters and photographers.

'I spoke to some of the reporters at the front door for a few minutes, then I had to force my way into the house. My wife had begun to get things marshalled and she'd started to plan what I ought to be doing. I was grateful that she had done what I hadn't been able to do. But I suppose it quickly dawned on me that there was a role that had to be played with regard to the Press and if that was to be played by any of the clergy in Dunblane then it would have to be me, simply because of the position the cathedral has.

'I probably realised that fairly early on, and that I would have to accept that role. So I suddenly found myself up in Wallace Road for quite a while giving interviews. I regret that now as it was a number of hours before I was able to start going round the homes of the bereaved parents.'

Colin and representatives from Dunblane's other churches met in the town's Churches House later that day.

'We just didn't know what to say to each other. We quickly began to realise just what lay ahead for us, as clergy, and I think we were very concerned that we wouldn't be able to cope with this. We'd been provided with a list of names. We just sat there in silence looking at it. The list was so long. Alongside the name of each child was their address. But what really got through to us were the dates of birth. They were all so young.

'It was a terrible task, but we had to clinically divide up the list of names. Some were obviously members of the respective churches, but there were a number who didn't belong to any church. They were divided up according to the parish system.

'I visited some of the families on my list later on that night, simply because I couldn't let the day end without having been there. But it was difficult getting on with the job because there was just so much pressure coming from the Press.'

At the meeting the clergy agreed to hold a vigil at the cathedral on the Friday night – two days after the massacre. The idea of the vigil came out very quickly and really quite spontaneously.

'We agreed that we had to be available for the people. I said that we couldn't just spend our time in the homes of the bereaved, we had to walk the streets. We had to be seen and be available to anyone. In fact, for the next two or three weeks I would set aside at least an hour of the day to walk up and down that High Street.

'We decided that there had to be an opportunity for the whole community to come together, and that it had to happen as soon as humanly possible, so the Friday-night vigil was suggested.

'But what we planned that night was different from what actually happened. We knew a lot of people would want to come, so we planned the service in 15-minute slots and we shared out the slots between all the clergy. That meant each of us would say prayers, then there would be a reading, a period of silence, then the organist would play, which would allow people to leave the cathedral and let others come in.

'We anticipated a large turnover of people, but we never anticipated the estimated 5,000 who came that night. So many people wanted to take part in the vigil we simply had to abandon our original timetable.

'We had originally planned the vigil to run from 7.30 p.m. until 9 p.m., but the people were still coming in at 10.45 p.m.'

Sheets of paper started to appear near the door of the cathedral. Soon they became a makeshift Book of Commemoration and people queued to sign it, desperate in some small way to leave a message, a mark of respect on this night of tears. Some just simply signed their name.

'I don't to this day know where the paper appeared from. We felt it was important for people to have the opportunity to write something, even if it was just a name. Some people even refused to leave the cathedral without signing it. There was a long queue to sign the book, but nobody seemed to bother. They were prepared to wait.

'A lot of truly remarkable things were happening in Dunblane, and I don't know how or why they did. I think it says something about the people here. Folk just appeared because they knew things would need to be done, and they knew they could do them.

'Some appeared because they realised that they actually could meet people, talk to people, cuddle them if necessary. Others knew they couldn't do that, but they could make a cup of tea, so they appeared in the church hall.

'For days on end the hall was open. I never had to ask anyone to open it. People just appeared and there was a constant supply of tea. Flowers began appearing, so people began arriving to arrange the flowers . . .

'Everything that took place over that time, nobody ever asked for it to be done. I've always felt that was a marvellous tribute to an awful lot of people.

'An office was set up in the manse, and I never asked for it to be done. A whole succession of elders from the cathedral came in to staff and man the telephone, and there was another small office set up at the front door. I could have my privacy in the study, but necessary work could still go on.

'Someone would come in and work for a couple of hours, then someone else would almost magically come along afterwards to take over. Nobody asked for it to be done, it just happened. At that time of year the cathedral normally closed at 4 p.m., but for the first few days after the tragedy it was still open at midnight.

'A lot of people were coming in. Some of them just wanted to come in and be on their own quietly. Some wanted to come in and walk around, others came because they wanted to talk and you had to be able to tell the difference between those who wanted to talk and those who didn't.'

But Colin found that much of the vital work he was able to do in these early days was on the streets of Dunblane.

'I think it was important that I walked around the streets where folk who might be reluctant to come inside the church were able to speak to me, and I made a point of doing that every day. I think that was very valuable as a great many people came up and spoke to me.

'Whether I was able to help people at the time I'm not sure. I was aware I had a job to do, a role to carry out, but I wasn't thinking: "I need to do this because I'm the minister here." It was just something that you do instinctively and spontaneously, because you're a human being.

'I can't even remember the things I was saying to people. I suspect I was doing more listening than talking and I think the important thing was just to share, rather than to have the right words to say to people. It was a sharing of emotions, and maybe that was actually more help to people.'

But the quiet, unassuming clergyman found himself thrust into a new role in these early days – dealing with the world's Press. As a local minister his only experience of journalists was speaking to the local weekly newspaper. He admits he wasn't prepared for the intense media attention centred on his town . . .

And he suffered his first real public display of emotion after an interview with ITN.

'I really cannot recall in detail which newspapers, television and radio journalists I spoke to and in what order, but I do remember sitting in the manse on the day of the shootings. ITN wanted a filmed interview and I can remember sitting here doing that. I can't remember a word I said, but it was after that I had my first reaction. I just went totally to pieces. The ITN reporter and film crew were really nice about it, but some of the interviews were tough to get through.

'I found it strange having to deal with the Press, realising that my words were probably going out worldwide. It's a totally different experience from standing with two parents on a one-to-one personal basis with them, speaking about their child. Perhaps I began to see there was another dimension to this, not only the personal tragedies, but the national and even the world dimension, which I don't think had crossed my mind at all. I suppose I thought it was a local situation, that this was something terrible that's happened in Dunblane and it's happened to people I know. But of course I really hadn't thought through all the implications. I hadn't realised that within hours the world would be represented here, focusing on this one little community and that in some way I was going to turn out to be one of the spokesmen.'

A CHURCHMAN

The community of Dunblane was to come together again on Sunday, 17 March – Mothering Sunday. Colin McIntosh sat down to try to find the words, the right words to say to a shattered community.

'I remember thinking: "How can you hold a service, how can you say something about God in this kind of situation?" But I didn't have time to worry about it, I didn't have time to think about it. I'd been so busy I wasn't able to start preparing my sermon until late on the Saturday night and most of it was done in the small hours of Sunday morning. You go on to automatic pilot. I simply drew on instinct. In these pressure situations your adrenalin flows and your reactions are much sharper. But I knew it had to be done, so I just sat down and did it. Within a few hours it was complete.

'Decisions had to be made about whether the service was to be televised or not. The BBC had been on to me for a day or two wanting to televise the whole thing and I took the decision that it would be right, because it had become clear that this wasn't just a local matter, this was something that was touching the whole world.'

On any other fourth Sunday in Lent, Dunblane Cathedral would have been a happy place. Mothering Sunday. A day to rejoice. A day to give. A day of peace and hope.

But the hundreds who gathered at the cathedral on 17 March sat in numbed silence, trying to make sense of the horror. Trying to come to terms with their grief.

With the front pews filled with children, many of whom had lost friends and playmates, Colin McIntosh's carefully chosen words rang out around these ancient walls. And the whole world listened . . .

'We are remembering every boy and girl in that class because we know how happy they were and how much fun they had together and how much their parents loved them and how unfair and wrong it all seems to be, and we don't understand it.

'Even the grown-ups don't understand why this has happened. Our only comfort lies in knowing that it was not the will of God that our children should die, that in those fatal, frightening moments in the school gym, God's heart was the first of all our hearts to break.

'The reality is that last Wednesday morning we glimpsed a facet of life that we don't ever dare to consider for too long. That what begins as an ordinary day for ordinary people, walking to the shops, meeting neighbours, taking our children to school, can end in such heartache, sorrow and despair. That it can happen to innocent children in school where they always felt happy and safe. And that not even the strongest words of faith can bypass the pain of loss and grief, or protect us from that awful sense we have that with the deaths of many of our children and their devoted teacher, something of our own life has lost its meaning.

'When our parents die, they take with them a large proportion of the past. But when our children die, they take away the future as well.'

Colin McIntosh then had the daunting task of helping to arrange funeral services for the victims.

'We had to co-ordinate the services so that bereaved parents could attend funerals of other children as well. We had to work out how they could be timed to allow this. It was clearly becoming important because one of the amazing things was that the parents were not just preoccupied with their own grief, they were thinking of other families as well. Some parents wanted to be at other funerals even if it was being held on the same day as their own child's funeral. Talk about courage.

'I was also determined to try to make all the services for which I was responsible, unique. I wanted to be able to say something that was true to that child or the teacher, so there was going to be no such thing as a standard funeral and that meant an awful lot more work.

'One of the ways I approached that was to ask the parents to force themselves to spend time putting down on paper some things about their child. We made sure that we set aside time for that, to sit down with them and just talk about their child. The arithmetic of suffering here was a problem and already we were talking about 17 deaths and it was important that we saw these as 17 unique individual lives and didn't just think of the sum. I hope we were able to achieve that to some extent and that the service was special for each person. I hope so. That was certainly one of the things I was very concerned about.'

The clergyman admits he has questioned his own faith over the last 12 months.

'Religious faith is something that I frequently question and sometimes doubt. I've had a few doubts in the past, but this has been the worst experience I've ever encountered. But I don't think I could have begun to cope or do anything I was able to do unless there was something even deeper than that questioning and that doubting. If there were times when I felt I had lost hold of anything I believed in, at the same time I had the sense that there was something holding me. For some reason I wasn't totally going to pieces and I was working with greater sharpness and efficiency and clarity than I had before. I wasn't worrying about myself. I wasn't thinking: "How am I going to cope with this? How am I going to face this?" These questions just didn't come into my mind at all, so whilst I was saying "God why, why?" there was something else, there was something deeper than this that was holding me.'

And Colin McIntosh believes he has changed as a person since the tragic events of last March.

'I don't think anyone could not have changed, but for me, I would be happier answering that question in five years' time. One of the difficulties I still have is I'm not sufficiently distant from it to be objective. I'm not detached as yet. I'm too close to it. There are a lot of films I cannot watch now; the violent ones, the ones that seem to glorify violence, I just cannot bear to look at them.

'I can't be in the presence of children without contradictory thoughts. I find myself thinking how wonderful it is to be with children, but it's combined with a sadness.'

And he believes that parents should not look upon the anniversary of the massacre as the last barrier they have to get over before somehow starting afresh, trying to get on with their lives.

'The last year has simply been a succession of hurdles. We've faced each hurdle knowing that beyond it there was yet another. Now I think the danger is that we look at 13 March as the last hurdle after which everything will get back to normal. The families may think that after they have surmounted the last hurdle, there won't be any others for them and that they will be able to get back to something like normality. I don't think that will be the case. I think they will find themselves struggling for a long, long time.

'I also have a concern that after 13 March the community as a whole will think that it's time to get back to normal. I think that will be false. The grieving in some ways will only begin for the first time after the anniversary, because there hasn't yet been the time or the space to do it.

'I hope that we will get some freedom from the Press. I can't think

149

of anything else that would make the Press want to come into Dunblane again. I hope we'll get a bit of space, but I think there will be many other difficulties ahead of a personal private kind.

'People should not think that from 14 March onwards everything will be all right.'

11. A MUSICIAN

THE BACKDROP was impressive. Stirling Castle in all its summer evening glory.

Halfway through the concert, members of the audience were invited up to the stage for a karaoke-style segment. Microphone in hand, musicians in the background, and off they went. One woman led up to the stage was wearing a long, black dress.

Singer, songwriter and international recording star Chris de Burgh was told she was 'connected' to the families, an aunt possibly. She took the mike, breathed in deeply and started to sing one of Chris's hits as he played guitar. The audience loved it – a standing ovation. Cheers and tears. Chris walked over to his piano and knew exactly where to find the handkerchief the sound technician had concealed – just in case.

He turned his back briefly on the five thousand or so in front of the stage overshadowed by the historical monument on the rock. It was Chris's turn for the deep breathing. A few seconds to regain composure. And on with the three-hour-long outdoor concert.

It was exactly what the Dunblane families had requested. It was just what the performer had wished for. To help. In his own way.

Last March on that fateful morning Chris did the school run with his three children from their home outside Dublin. It takes around 45 minutes in total. He was between concert tours and was catching up with colleagues on the telephone.

'I travel so much in my business, so whenever I'm at home I like to take the children to their schools in the morning. Just before noon I was speaking to Pat Savage, a colleague in London. He'd recently become a father so he was filling me in on all that. Then he asked if I'd heard the news about what had happened in a school in Scotland. At that stage Dunblane hadn't even been mentioned.

'I switched on the television and the news came on. If there was ever a case of saying my jaw fell slack, this was it. I stood there in the room, tears pouring down my face. I gripped and ungripped my fists in rage and I couldn't believe what I was hearing. I was terribly upset. The references to the little children – at that point there were 13 feared dead. I couldn't take it all in.

'At about 1 p.m. my wife Diane arrived home with our five-year-old son Michael and two of his school friends. They burst in through the door like a hurricane. They ran around, making noise – just like five-year-olds should. I grabbed Michael, took him quietly aside and just held him. He was wriggling about trying to get away to see his friends, but honestly I had to hold him tightly.

'I took Diane into the front room and again I cried as I told her about the reports coming in. We both watched TV. We were both utterly shocked. I went into another room and started hitting things in rage. I don't know why. Strong emotions are aroused by having children. There's that primeval rush of emotion and a desire to protect and nurture, to cherish and look after and obviously protect them from any harm.

'At that point Dunblane meant nothing to me. I'm sure I'd heard of it because I've done a number of concerts in Scotland but primarily in the Edinburgh, Glasgow and Aberdeen triangle. I'd been to Stirling before and I have an aunt who lived in Pittenweem in Fife and I used to go up there regularly.

'As the TV news coverage developed, the full horror grew before my eyes. I noticed a police helpline number and jotted down a note of it. By that time I had recovered a bit from the initial overwhelming shock, but my feelings for the parents, naturally, and for the other members of their families, were of complete empathy. I kept thinking, how would I feel? How would I even begin to handle a tragedy like this?

'About an hour later I decided to telephone the helpline number. A girl answered. I told her I was certain she'd been inundated with calls, but I just wanted it put on record that I called to offer my help. I said my name and she said: "I know who you are."

'I told her I didn't want to interfere but said I would be keen to do something to help the community. I mentioned that some of my songs are about children and have provided comfort to many people who have been in great distress. I didn't expect someone to get back to me this year, next year or next century, if at all, but I wanted it recorded that if I could help I would. I'm a singer and I know songs can provide comfort. That's the sort of help I could offer. She took my name and details.'

The following weekend press coverage – and in particular the photographs, including the class picture – hit Chris hard.

'I could hardly bear to read it and I could hardly bear to look at the picture of the man responsible. It was his smug, smiling-like face staring out from the page. I could barely think about the details of what he had done and how he had done it. Here was a man responsible for the rape of childhood and the rape of a community because he had guns. I used to go to America often and lived in California for six months. The gun culture there for me is abhorrent and it is not a country that I am comfortable taking my family to. I remember I was walking down the street in New York years ago with my wife after a dinner and a guy walked down the street firing a revolver. Bang. Bang. Bang. Your chances of being randomly killed by gunfire in America are enormous. Wherever you have a right to carry weapons – as in the States – you're just asking for trouble.

'So the idea of anything like this happening in a normal little town, in a God-fearing part of Scotland, was so difficult to comprehend.

'I wept looking at that class picture. I looked at them and I thought, God these are all golden little kiddies. A lot of them seemed to have gold, blond hair. They looked angelic. The teacher looked such a lovely lady standing there with all these little angels. We have photographs like that one from school. Every parent has. They usually take pride of place in the children's rooms. I thought, Jesus this is just like any school picture. Anywhere. They're all smiling and happy. It was unbearable to look at them. One paper detailed each child from the picture. It then hit me just how much grief was instantly involved. Hundreds of people grieving for each one because they knew the child personally.'

Chris had enjoyed international success with a string of 14 albums to his credit and his biggest hit with the song 'Lady in Red'. He performs live regularly throughout the world.

About four months after his initial call Chris was in the middle of a UK tour. During a break he was back home in Ireland. A call came to his London office from Central Scotland Police. Chief Constable Willie Wilson wanted to speak with him.

'I remember it well. It was the third day of the Irish Golf Open at Druids Glen. I'm a member there and on my way to the club I rang the office. They told me about the call. I phoned back and the message was that the families were positive about me doing something. I felt a concert could be a focus for the community. It had been totally shattered by the event. The awful thing here was that the perpetrator had killed himself so that was not a focus. There was not a focus for anger before or after the funerals and church services, nor a focus for grief and coming together. I had thought about a concert exclusively for the families – perhaps in a church or some hall somewhere in Dunblane.

'Even though it was just four months after the event I was surprised the families had responded so soon. I was in the middle of the UK tour and we'd been playing places like Blenheim Palace and Hampton Court Palace. We had a full orchestra. There was the suggestion of doing some kind of musical event, a proper concert to raise funds for the Dunblane Appeal which had been set up. I explained to Mr Wilson that normally organising a concert would take up to four months. This time we had just two weeks in which to put the whole event together. The idea was simple. An open-air concert on the esplanade at Stirling Castle.

'I spoke to my production manager Steve Martin and my manager, Scotsman Kenny Thomson, and they got on the case right away. They pulled so many strokes to make it happen. In fact the whole thing was organised in less than two weeks. There was a huge amount of goodwill directed towards the event. People gave their services free. Sound systems appeared free of charge. The security people helped out. I wasn't sure how much money we'd raise, but that wasn't the main priority. We wanted the families to come together for an evening of music. Most came, and between five and six thousand people turned out.

'The day before the concert I'd been in Disneyland Paris with my family. I told the children what was coming next and that it was very important to be there together.

'We flew to Scotland and the night before the concert I met the police who showed us around their headquarters in Stirling; they were very considerate and hospitable.

'There had been criticism of the police. I was very much aware of that point. I felt I wanted to put myself above all that. I was there simply to do a concert out of respect for the families affected.'

At the time Chris was stung by one journalist who suggested he was doing the concert to raise his own profile. At the time he said: 'If anybody has the guts to say it to my face, I will hit them as hard as I possibly can. For years I've been known as a person who supports children's charities.

'This was a simple human response to a human tragedy. I am a performer, and singing and concerts are what I do best. I got involved because the people most directly affected wanted me to. That was very important.'

A one minute's silence was scheduled for the concert. Local MP and Scots Secretary Michael Forsyth and MP George Robertson who lives in Dunblane attended the concert with their families. The concert was expected to raise around £25,000.

'On the night of the concert the conditions were perfect. The sun set directly on to the stage and the scene was set.

'Prior to going on stage all the families gathered at the Stirling Highland Hotel a few minutes' walk from the castle. I remember vividly walking into the room with Diane and my children. There were about 50 people. I was apprehensive, probably nervous about meeting them all. All the families were in small groups. One group per family. All rather isolated in the room. I went round each group, chatting and introducing my family. I asked each group what was their association to the school. One by one they told their stories. I couldn't believe what I was hearing. Courageously they explained if their child had been killed or injured.

'I remember there was a little girl in a wheelchair and she had a leg brace on. Gosh, she was pretty, full of sparkle and life. I bent down and chatted to her for a while.

'At that point I left the room. To be honest I couldn't stand it any longer. I was so upset. I remember walking down the hotel corridor hitting the wall as hard as I could, in rage and frustration. How could anybody do that? What kind of hate does a man have in him to commit the murders? I composed myself, came back in again after five minutes and I saw my wife was very upset as well.

'But we talked on. I remember meeting Dr Mick North, whose daughter Sophie was shot. He thanked me for meeting them. And he said that a lot of people had been too scared to meet them, too scared to speak to them because they simply didn't know what to say. The families were feeling like outcasts because people didn't feel comfortable about approaching them. I could see his point. How do you approach people in a tragedy like this? I was looking at them clear-eyed and saying this is something I can do.'

One of the songs Chris performed that night was 'Carry Me Like a Fire in Your Heart'.

'I wrote it for a friend of mine, Mark Kavanagh, who lost his wife. I remember after her death he was having problems grieving, letting himself go. I wrote the song in about two days, which is very fast for me. After the funeral there were 20 or 30 close friends with him and I sang the song. I said it was my gift of love for Mark and his children.

'I recorded the track in 1988 and I remember going round to see Mark with one of the first copies. Subsequently he told me that he and his children listened to it repeatedly and it was their emotional release.'

Here are the lyrics written by Chris.

There is an answer, some day we will know,
And you will ask her, why she had to go,
We live and die, we laugh and we cry,
And you must take away the pain,
Before you can begin to live again;

So let it start, my friend, let it start,
Let the tears come rolling from your heart,
And when you need a light in the lonely night,
Carry me like a fire in your heart,
Carry me like a fire in your heart;

There is a river rolling to the sea,
You will be with her for all eternity,
But we that remain need you here again.

So hold her in your memory,
And begin to make the shadows disappear;

Yes, let it start, my friend, let it start,
Let the tears come rolling from your heart,
And when you need a light in the lonely night,
Carry me like a fire in your heart,
Carry me like a fire in your heart;

And when you need a light in the lonely night,
Carry me like a fire in your heart,
Carry me like a fire in your heart.

'I knew that a lot of my songs have in the past provided a kind of release and comfort. I know from the letters I get from all over the world. The lyrics seem to have a lot of meaning for many, many people.

'During the actual concert I was apprehensive because I had to walk a very thin line between acknowledging what was happening that evening and acknowledging the fact it was entertainment as well. I didn't want it to be a depressing affair. It was about as difficult a balance as I've ever had to make in my entire professional career and I have done thousands of concerts. This one for me was quite possibly going to be the most difficult.

'I asked my guitar technician to hide a handkerchief because I thought I might need it. When you're a singer, your throat closes if you're crying. You can't sing and it's very painful so I knew I had to control myself. I noticed people reacting to lines in songs. I glanced round at Steve, the production boss, who spent most of the concert in tears. He had clicked into the enormity of the occasion for the families and it kept hitting him.

'During my concerts there is a point which I laughingly refer to as the "karaoke bit". I invite members of the audience to come and sing anything. Some sing dreadfully badly and others sing really well. It's all part of the show and people love it. I think at Stirling a couple of girls stood up and sang. Then I noticed a man and a young lady coming down. She was wearing a black dress. The man asked if this young lady could sing. I'm sure he said she was an aunt or close friend of one of

157

the victims. She took the microphone with trembling hands. I sat at the side of the stage and she sang a song of mine called "Where Peaceful Waters Flow". She sang it very well. At the end of the song everybody stood up. It was a tidal wave of emotions. Like petrol igniting. Everybody was in tears.

'Then I walked to the piano, took the handkerchief and wiped my own tears. It was a beautiful moment but it was like being kicked in the stomach.

'I did some of my more light-hearted numbers and stuff like "Spanish Train" and "Patricia the Stripper". The concert ended and there was a great response. I knew where the families were sitting in the audience. I saw them smiling. I saw them laughing.

'Afterwards I had a quick shower and went to meet the families again. The change from what we'd seen before was brilliant. The first thing I saw was Mick North walking around with four glasses of wine, doing his waiter bit, and he was laughing and cheerful. Everyone seemed up. All the individual groups had gone, everyone was mingling. It was amazing. The rest of the evening was fantastic and we stayed on chatting for ages.'

The next day Chris and his family had made up their minds to go to Dunblane cemetery.

'I'd spoken to Gwen Mayor's husband Rod about it and we told him we would like to see it before we left for home. We drove up from Stirling, parked at the gates and walked in. The sight of all these graves together was so overpowering. One of the gravestones was in the shape of a teddy bear. All, of course, had the date 13 March inscribed. One child had the same birth date as my little niece. They both would have been exactly the same age.'

Chris and his wife attended the special memorial service held in Dunblane Cathedral.

'It was such a sad service, hearing each child's name read out as their families lit a candle. I looked up at one point and I saw the little girl I'd met at the concert in Stirling. She was waving at me from down the aisle. That did two things to me. One, it made me dreadfully sad. But it also made me happy that she'd remembered me. She'd seen all the horrors of that day, and yet she could still be cheery. That really lifted my heart.

'Following the service we made another visit to the cemetery. This time most of the gravestones had been erected. It's beyond belief to see that little corner of the graveyard.

'After the memorial service, I said to one of the fathers that I was struggling to understand, but I could just about imagine what they were going through. He stopped me immediately. He said: "You cannot imagine what it is like. You cannot have any concept of what it's like." And he was right.

'It was a very humbling experience to be among this group of people who had all suffered and endured such tragedy and also to see how they turned to each other for help.'

In November secret preparations were made for Chris to appear at an awards ceremony in Glasgow. The *Sunday Mail* newspaper's annual Great Scots ceremony pays tribute to the good and the great of the country.

The judging panel headed by respected High Court judge Lord McCluskey had decided to give the top award not to one individual but to the entire community of Dunblane and those involved in the aftermath of the tragedy.

Announcing the award, Lord McCluskey said: 'This year in Scotland was dominated by one horrifying and numbing tragedy. The images made each of us sob with frustration and grief. Countless words have been spoken and written about these events and the waste of it all. We do not seek to find new words. We did not presume to select one person as more deserving than any other, though many were nominated to us for individual recognition. We simply wanted to mark the fact that everyone in Scotland shares in the overwhelming sadness of the loss. If there is one aspect of this tragedy that has humbled us all, it is the dignity with which the people of Dunblane have borne their suffering.'

He added that the award was 'an inadequate but heartfelt tribute to the dignity in suffering of those whom we now recognise as the greatest of Scots'.

The award was received on behalf of the community by the Reverend Colin McIntosh of Dunblane Cathedral.

As the ceremony drew to a close, Chris was introduced to the 500-strong audience. He then performed a number of his hits including 'Carry Me Like a Fire in Your Heart'.

Four bereaved parents had been specially invited to attend the ceremony. Chris met them briefly before the ceremony began.

'I knew where they were sitting, but few others in the hall knew who they were, and that's what they'd wanted. As I sang, I could see their table and I realised emotions were running high. I finished my performance, walked from the stage right over to their table and gave them a big hug. I could hear the sobs. It was my moment of doing a little to help, to try and comfort them. It was a very emotional point.'

For Chris the impact of Dunblane lives on – and he expects it will remain with him for the rest of his life.

'The echoes from Dunblane will reverberate for ever. I can't look at young children any more without thinking about Dunblane. I find it difficult to look at school photographs, even of my own youngsters. Instantly I think of that class and Mrs Mayor.

'It's not an obsession with me and it's not because I'm that close to what happened, but, having met the families, I now have some inkling of the huge emotional devastation caused by that incident.

'I get very emotional – and always have done – when children are involved in bad or difficult situations. If children are affected then it's guaranteed to get me all misty-eyed. The Dunblane incident was just so powerful. It's been an irresistible force and still something that gets me deeply upset.

'Unfortunately if you mention Dunblane in Russia, Alaska or Patagonia, most people know what happened. Whether this is an instrument for change or not, I don't know. It's certainly been a milestone in many people's lives, including my own, and one that will never be forgotten.

'I want to retain my friendship and contact with the people involved, and I think it makes you remember that the reason we are on the planet is to have children, protect them, bring them with help and love out of the nest until they can fly unaided, and be there for them when they require assistance after they have left the nest.'

When Chris and Diane are on that school run now, the legacy of Dunblane is with them when they see their son Michael into his classes.

'At the door there is a security system and you have to punch in numbers on a pad before the door opens. That was an immediate response to what happened. The man involved in Dunblane is responsible for that. These security measures are repeated not just here in Ireland and the UK but in places all over the world. Now, hopefully, someone with a grudge can't just wander into a school as before and commit some dreadful act.

'The images of a class of 16 pupils and their teacher wiped out and their classmates and other staff left badly injured, burn into my memory.'

In Chris's bedroom at home a little green trinket box sits on a table. He treasures its contents. A pair of specially-commissioned silver cuff-links – crafted in the shape of snowdrops – sent to him by a group of the families at Christmas. A token of their gratitude.

'I was stunned when they arrived. I'm going to wear them at a very special event. I wrote to say thank you and say how honoured I was to receive them.

'I don't want them to regard me as anything else than a friend, a person who did help and can help.'

One comment sticks with Chris from the last year during his involvement with the Dunblane people. He and his family had arrived at Edinburgh Airport and a TV news team asked for some reaction to the tragedy.

'Asked what he thought, my eight-year-old son Hubie said: "It's not fair. The children only had five years to live. It's really not fair . . ."

'It was a child's simple, beautiful little comment that summed it all up.'

12. A CHILD

HE bounds into the house, his mass of blond hair all ruffled by the winter breeze, and heads straight for his bedroom . . .

In one seemingly effortless motion he tosses his schoolbag in the corner while impatiently pulling off his school shirt and trousers.

Like a mini-human whirlwind leaving a trail of clothes in his wake, he begins searching frantically through his chest of drawers . . .

Seconds later little Coll Austin emerges triumphantly from the room, bedecked head-to-toe in his beloved Scotland strip, ball tucked neatly under arm, and shouts:

'Time for football, Dad. First to twenty!'

Coll Austin is a little boy any dad would be proud of. Polite. Caring. Considerate. A right 'little man' at only six years old who isn't afraid to show his love for his mum and dad and little brother and sister.

As he runs about tirelessly in the garden, his little legs pumping as he tries to dribble the ball round his dad, it's hard to believe that 12 months ago Coll lay bleeding and close to death on the floor of Dunblane Primary School gym.

He watched in terror as his schoolchums died. He ran for his life. He was hunted down by the 'smiling' gunman . . . But against all the odds, he survived.

Now Coll Austin has a dream which would melt the heart. He has told his mum and dad he wants a pair of time shoes so he can travel back in time – a bit like the car in the movie *Back to the Future*.

'He says he would go and get his wee pals,' says his dad. 'He would get John and David and Brett first. Then he would go back for everybody else before the man came.'

Coll Austin has witnessed a living hell which no human should have to bear. His childhood innocence has been tainted by the horrors of Wednesday, 13 March.

But he is surrounded by love now. He can nestle under his mum and dad's protective wing. He's warm and secure in their country home just outside Dunblane.

He left that same safe haven as usual on the morning of 13 March. Giving his mum and dad a peck on the cheek, he dashed out of the house, slipping on the icy path as he made his way towards the taxi for school.

'It could have been the last time we saw him alive,' dad Joe and mum Rona reflected.

The couple tell Coll's terrible story with clarity and emotion. Over the last year the youngster has given them an amazing insight into exactly what happened in the gym on that day of tears.

Coll had been happily warming up with his classmates in the gym when the gunman came bursting in the door.

One of the first bullets hit Coll in the foot, but the youngster turned and ran with a limp which made him look as if he was galloping. He headed for the gym storeroom where he thought he could hide . . . But he never made it.

With an evil look, the gunman followed Coll, aimed his pistol and fired another bullet into his back. He fell on to the floor, face down.

Coll lay helpless and bleeding while the gunman fired at his schoolchums before leaving the gym through an emergency door . . .

But the nightmare wasn't over for little Coll. The gunman came back into the gym and noticed he was still alive. He walked up to Coll, so close that the six year old could clearly see the details on his boots, and fired another bullet into his back to finish him off.

Coll had been shot four times – once in the foot, twice in the back and once through the arm. He suffered two collapsed lungs and broken ribs. One of the bullets entered his back and exited into his head, breaking his jaw and fracturing his cheekbone. He has lost sight and hearing on his right side.

He had to be resuscitated on the gym floor by paramedics before being flown by air ambulance helicopter to Yorkhill children's hospital in Glasgow.

Joe and wife Rona stayed at their son's bedside for three days before he regained consciousness. Throughout, he was on a life support machine.

As he opened his eyes he immediately began telling his mum and dad his amazing story.

'He tried to speak straight away,' said Joe. 'He was still on a ventilator and so he couldn't talk properly.

'The first thing I remember him doing was staring at me and using sign language. He began pointing his finger gun-style at his chest. He became very distressed and was crying. The doctors increased his sedation.

'On the fourth day, I'll never forget the first thing he said. In a whisper, he told us Mrs Mayor was dead and that everybody else was dead. He said he couldn't go back to school because his teacher had been killed. He thought the whole class was dead.

'He said he'd tried to make his way to the storeroom where Mrs Harrild had gone and that when he was running everybody else was lying down. He thought they had all been killed.

'He'd been shot in the foot and he was literally galloping towards the storeroom. Then Coll fell, and the next thing he remembered was looking at one of his friends, Robert Purves, who was just inside the storeroom.

'I think Coll thought Robert was dead, because he was just staring towards Coll, surrounded by blood.

'As he was lying down staring at Robert, he doesn't remember being shot again. But we think the gunman had gone out of the gym and come back in again. He must have seen Coll moving. He walked to within six feet of where Coll was and shot him in the back again. Coll can remember clearly seeing the man's feet. He can remember in fine detail the boots he had on. The final shot caused extensive injuries.

'The next thing Coll remembers is speaking to Linda Stewart, one of his nursery teachers. He remembers asking her to help him. He says he was trying to lift his head up to see her. Then John Currie, the school janitor, stayed with Coll until the paramedics arrived. It was John who drew their attention to Coll, because they were busy trying to find out who was still alive and who was dead. John had been sitting with Coll trying to keep him awake by asking him questions. Coll says he can remember John saying to him: "Haud on wee man, we'll get you out of here." When the paramedics arrived, Coll had stopped breathing. John grabbed one of them and said Coll was slipping away and they were able to bring him round.

'Coll said he was lying on the floor speaking to John and he remembers the doctor's tie because it had a pattern which had little pizza shapes on it.

'He recalls that the doctor kept calling him Paul. Coll was getting angrier and angrier, but the doctor was doing it on purpose, teasing him to keep him awake. He didn't want him to lose consciousness.'

When Joe and Rona arrived at hospital to see Coll, his mum didn't recognise him at first as his head and chest were very badly swollen. He had so many dressings on his face, neck and body.

'The situation was dire,' recalled Joe. 'The newspapers at the time said there was one of the victims who was giving doctors cause for concern. That was Coll.

'The doctors never offered any hope really. They reckoned it was touch and go whether he would make it or not. They wouldn't even say if he had a 50-50 chance. They didn't really think he would make it through the first night. It was pretty desperate. We were told that one of the medics on the helicopter said he wouldn't have given tuppence for Coll's chances.

'They thought that his injuries were so severe there were any number of things that could kill him, such as infections or respiratory distress. There were a whole load of complications. The bereavement counsellor came in to speak to us, and I remember asking him if we could take Coll home if he died.'

Joe and Rona spent three days at Coll's bedside, holding his hand, talking to him, praying he would open his eyes.

'We were with him every single moment we could stay awake. I just kept on chatting to him,' said Joe. 'I remember he was into football stickers at the time, so I was buying packets of them, taking them into the hospital and opening them in front of him, telling him which ones he'd got. I just tried to talk normally to him. I thought, if he could hear me, he would find it a comfort just knowing we were there for him.'

When Coll did wake up, Joe had the heartbreaking task of telling his son which of his classmates had died and who had survived.

'He thought everybody was dead and we had to explain to him that wasn't the case. He was quite adamant that everyone was dead because that's what he thought he'd seen when he was running around the gym.

'I had a newspaper with me with the Primary One class photograph in it. The names of the children were above their pictures and it stated whether they were dead or injured. I just went through it with him, pointing at every child one by one. I was worried it would appear cruel, but I didn't see any point in hiding the facts from him. I wanted to be honest with him. I was trying to think of a way to minimise the impact it would have on him, but it was impossible.

'When we were going through the class photograph, Coll was very quiet, very calm. He just looked at it. He recognised the word "dead", but "injured" was a new word to him and I had to explain what that meant.

'Then he said: "What about the man who did this, what happened to him?" I told him he was dead. Coll nodded and said: "That's fair."'

Amazingly, Coll was discharged from Yorkhill after only eight days – on the same day the Princess Royal came to visit.

'Princess Anne was due at the hospital and we told Coll she was the Queen's daughter. We asked him if he wanted to meet her and he said: "No, I want to go home, but she can have one of my jellyfish sweets if she wants." So Coll wrapped up a sweetie and sent a note to Princess Anne saying: "I want to go home, but thanks for coming to see me. Here's a jellyfish for you."

'He was delighted when he got a reply on Buckingham Palace notepaper saying: "Thanks for the jellyfish. It was good."

'Some people thought he was discharged too quickly, but the doctors weighed up the whole situation. They thought that psychologically the best place for Coll was in his own home, in his own bedroom. They wanted him back in familiar surroundings. They thought that any supervision Coll needed could be done at home.

'At first he wouldn't sleep and he didn't want to be on his own. So we would let him fall asleep on the couch and then carry him to bed.

'But he had been desperate to get home, just to get back. He'd been spoiled in hospital because he was allowed a room with a video and plenty of coke and fizzy juice and chocolate. He was loving it, but it was getting too much for him and he was just desperate to get back to normal. He needed the stability of being at home.'

When Dunblane Primary School reopened, Coll told his mum and dad he wanted to go back for a visit.

'He wanted to go back the first day it reopened,' said Joe. 'He only went for an hour. I think he just wanted to make sure the school was still there. Some of his friends who had survived were also there.'

Coll also asked his dad to take him to the gym.

'He was annoyed when he counted the bunches of flowers in the gym. He wanted there to be 17, but I think there were only about 12 that day. We were quite surprised that he wanted to go to the gym, although I suppose it was a healthy thing to want to do. He didn't see it as some kind of nightmare. It was HIS gym and he wasn't scared to go into it. I think a lot of adults would have been.

'The strange thing is John Currie, the janitor, was showing us round, and he didn't realise it was Coll. He didn't even know Coll had survived. It eventually dawned on him. You could see it in his face. It was so touching. Coll told John: "It was you who told me to hold on." Then he realised. He just looked at Coll, stared at him. He was really taken aback. He couldn't believe Coll was alive.'

Coll suffered a major setback in April when he had to go back into hospital to be treated for a collapsed lung which put pressure on his heart and affected his other lung. He spent almost three weeks in Yorkhill hospital.

But it wasn't long before he was fighting fit again, and back home beside his mum and dad.

Joe believes that although Coll seems to have coped with the trauma of the last year, there are still times when he sees marked changes in his son.

'Sometimes he gets very irritated. If he spills a drink on his blind side he says that it's HIS fault. He says: "It's his fault I spilled my drink because I can't see properly."

'Another time his little sister told him she had seen something scary. Coll turned round and snapped at her: "You don't know what it's like to be scared. I know what it's like to be scared." These flashpoints don't happen very often.

'He hasn't changed dramatically. It has obviously affected him, but it's difficult to measure. It's hard to separate normal childhood development and behaviour. It would be easy to blame any troubles Coll ever has on what happened to him.

'He has a healthy outlook on life. He has a balanced view of other people, he's kind and he shares things with other kids. If he has £1 in his pocket and his wee pal doesn't, he'll buy him a football comic. In most ways he is the same little boy as he was before March, but there are some differences in him. He's certainly more insecure about things. It is impossible to measure exactly how he has changed, but it sometimes comes through in things he says or things he'll do.

'For example, this morning he didn't want to go to school because sometimes he thinks that when the bell goes the whole place is going to go on fire. He thinks something bad will happen again.

'He once got very annoyed when we noticed he had hearing problems and arranged for him to see a specialist. He examined Coll and told him he was deaf and would need to be more protective of his other ear. He said he would have to be careful doing certain things and playing certain sports – like rugby and football – in case he got a bump on the head. Coll was irritated by this. He couldn't understand why someone was telling him he couldn't play a certain sport. That's good in a way because it shows he has a fighting spirit.

'And he certainly hasn't let his injuries stand in his way. He's certainly more cautious than he was. When he's playing football, he guards the side of his head. But he doesn't let it hold him back from doing anything.'

It was a slow process persuading Coll it was 'safe' for him to go back to school.

'It took him two months to settle back at school. When he first went back, I stayed with him in the mornings, sitting at the back of the class. He just wanted to make sure I was still around. There were a number of other parents in the same situation. If his class were moving around the school for any reason he wanted me with him. That situation diminished the more he realised that nothing out of the ordinary was going to happen. Eventually I was just walking him as far as the cloakroom, and since the beginning of January he's been going into the school himself. It's taken a long time to get to that stage. It's been a long slow process.'

Coll's injuries are a permanent reminder to Joe and Rona that this atrocity was caused by a man carrying a legally-held handgun.

'We've never given Coll toy guns to play with. He even knew that if a programme came on the television with lots of guns and violence in it he'd come and say: "We'll have to turn it over, there are guns in it." Even if he wanted to watch a particular programme, he wouldn't because there were guns in it. He knew our standards. He knew guns were real and dangerous and not toys. He knew guns were bad.'

When Joe looks at Coll's injuries today, they only serve to reinforce his anti-gun views.

'I have to keep remembering that Coll is one of the lucky ones. On 13 March I would have taken him back in any condition, maimed in any shape or form. When it gets right down to the basics, I was just glad to get to Yorkhill and hold his hand because he was still breathing, that's how bad it was. So several times a week now Rona and I cuddle him with that sort of awareness. It's quite overwhelming, especially when you realise how some parents are feeling and what they are going through. He is just so lucky to be here. Often after he's gone to sleep, I'll creep through and give him a little cuddle. All the time you are thinking: "He might not have been here." We feel lucky to have Coll. Other parents will never have the opportunity of seeing their loved ones come through the door again.

'Coll's been particularly lucky because of the nature of his injuries. One of the doctors said if you had to choose a path for a bullet to go through a head, then you would choose the way that bullet went. It just missed his brain. He said it was nothing short of a miracle.

'One doctor said that the recovery power of children should never be underestimated, but I think on this occasion they were absolutely astounded. He really won through against all the odds.'

Coll talks openly about the little pals he lost on that terrible morning in the gym.

'He really misses his friends,' says Joe. 'He often talks about them. And I'll often tell bereaved parents that Coll has been thinking about their son or daughter. It does give some comfort.

'It was so touching when he said that he wished he had a pair of time shoes so that he could travel in time. He says he would go and get his friends and bring them back, then he would go back and get the rest of the class.

'For adults it is impossible to forget what has happened, but a child has the ability to put things to the back of their mind, not to the point they can't discuss it, but they can always prioritise so much better.

'As adults we allow things to dominate us and churn us up, whereas children of that age don't. They just get on with life.

'When Coll and some of the other injured children get together they talk about their friends who died, but in a nice way. They won't let them be forgotten.'

Coll Austin's story is one of hope amid the death and destruction. He symbolises the bright light at the end of a long dark tunnel for the people of Dunblane. And, although he's only six years old, little Coll already has big dreams.

'When he grows up he wants to play football in Holland for Ajax and then AC Milan because he says football there is better than in Scotland. Once he's a top-class footballer, he wants to come back and play for Celtic and Scotland,' smiled Joe.

Little Coll Austin has defied the odds already. You wouldn't bet against him doing it again.

Coll keeps a book of drawings in his bedroom – one child's pictures and images of what happened on that darkest of days . . .

Alongside that book now is a cassette tape. Coll recorded it in his room one day in January. His voice strikes a chill into the heart . . .

'I miss my friends,' it crackles. 'I miss all my friends.'

A CHARITY

IT was the appalling plight of starving Austrian children, victims of a blockade after the First World War, that drove one dedicated woman to pioneer a campaign which challenged views across the world.

Eglantyne Jebb's resolve to put children first – above race, creed or nationality – led to the launch of Save the Children in 1919, the first of the modern development agencies.

Her ideas were a unique mix of the visionary and the practical, and far ahead of their time. She believed that to abolish the suffering born of poverty, conflict and deprivation, children's needs have to be met, not just in times of crisis, but 'by placing in their hands the means of saving themselves'.

Save the Children has always stayed true to these essential goals – emergency relief is not enough. Long-term programmes have to begin, so families can support themselves.

The scope of Eglantyne Jebb's international vision and her passionate conviction proved impossible to ignore.

The breakthrough came in 1924 when the declaration of children's rights, which she had drafted a year earlier, was adopted by the League of Nations. This charter has been the foundation of Save the Children's beliefs and actions ever since.

Since 1919, Save the Children has worked in more than 130 countries, for what Eglantyne Jebb set in motion made so much sense it ensured her principles survived the test of time.

In 1970 HRH The Princess Royal, Princess Anne, became President of Save the Children. The Queen is the charity's patron.

In the 1990s, Save the Children continues to work at the grassroots and is also in contact with international donors, influencing decision-makers concerning the foreign debt many developing countries face, and exploring ways of adjusting repayments. Save the Children is also pressing for major changes in the way the international community responds to emergencies and leading research into types of health care which communities can run themselves.